Information Concerning Dumping And Unfair Competition In The United States And Canada's Anti-dumping Law

You are holding a reproduction of an original work that is in the public domain in the United States of America, and possibly other countries. You may freely copy and distribute this work as no entity (individual or corporate) has a copyright on the body of the work. This book may contain prior copyright references, and library stamps (as most of these works were scanned from library copies). These have been scanned and retained as part of the historical artifact.

This book may have occasional imperfections such as missing or blurred pages, poor pictures, errant marks, etc. that were either part of the original artifact, or were introduced by the scanning process. We believe this work is culturally important, and despite the imperfections, have elected to bring it back into print as part of our continuing commitment to the preservation of printed works worldwide. We appreciate your understanding of the imperfections in the preservation process, and hope you enjoy this valuable book.

UNITED STATES TARIFF COMMISSION

INFORMATION

CONCERNING

DUMPING AND UNFAIR FOREIGN COMPETITION IN THE UNITED STATES

AND

CANADA'S ANTI-DUMPING LAW

Printed for the use of the Committee on Ways and Means
House of Representatives

WASHINGTON
GOVERNMENT PRINTING OFFICE
1919

COMMITTEE ON WAYS AND MEANS.

HOUSE OF REPRESENTATIVES.

SIXTY-SIXTH CONGRESS, FIRST SESSION.

JOSEPH W. FORDNEY, Michigan, *Chairman.*

J. HAMPTON MOORE, Pennsylvania.	CHARLES B. TIMBERLAKE, Colorado.
WILLIAM R. GREEN, Iowa.	GEORGE M. BOWERS, West Virginia.
NICHOLAS LONGWORTH, Ohio.	CLAUDE KITCHIN, North Carolina.
WILLIS C. HAWLEY, Oregon.	HENRY T. RAINEY, Illinois.
ALLEN T. TREADWAY, Massachusetts.	CORDELL HULL, Tennessee.
IRA C. COPLEY, Illinois.	JOHN N. GARNER, Texas.
LUTHER W. MOTT, New York.	JAMES W. COLLIER, Mississippi.
GEORGE M. YOUNG, North Dakota.	CLEMENT C. DICKINSON, Missouri.
JAMES A. FREAR, Wisconsin.	WILLIAM A. OLDFIELD, Arkansas.
JOHN Q. TILSON, Connecticut.	CHARLES R. CRISP, Georgia.
ISAAC BACHARACH, New Jersey.	JOHN F. CAREW, New York.
LINDLEY H. HADLEY, Washington.	WHITMELL P. MARTIN, Louisiana.

ERNEST W. CAMP, *Clerk.*

CONTENTS.

	Page.
Letter of transmittal	5
Introduction	7
CHARACTERISTICS OF DUMPING AND CERTAIN OTHER FOREIGN COMPETITIVE PRACTICES	9
Dumping	9
Foreign grants and bounties and countervailing duties	10
Full line forcing	10
Simultaneous sacrifice sales at home and abroad	10
Severe competition	11
Deceptive use of trade-marks, imitation of goods and advertising; false labeling; exploitation of patents; commercial threats and bribery	11
Undervaluation and additional duties	11
THE TARIFF COMMISSION'S INQUIRY IN THE UNITED STATES	12
Instances reported to the commission	13
Indications of dumping	13
Instances of severe competition	15
Charges of deceptive imitation of goods; false labeling; and deceptive use of trade-marks	16
Complaints of undervaluation	17
COMMENTS ON RESULTS OF THE COMMISSION'S INQUIRY	18
Fair and unfair competitive methods to be distinguished	18
Difficulty of proving dumping	18
Explanation of dumping practices	19
Intent as an element in dumping	20
CANADA'S ANTI-DUMPING LAW	21
The Tariff Commission's investigation in Canada	21
Canada's original anti-dumping provision enacted in 1904	21
Reasons assigned for Canada's legislation of 1904	22
Canadian tariff hearings in 1905–6	24
Administration of the anti-dumping clause of 1904	24
The 1904 clause opposed by farmers and importers	24
The 1904 clause indorsed in 1905–6 by manufacturing industries	25
Canada's anti-dumping clause, as amended in 1907, and now in force	25
Amendments of 1907	26
Administration of the present Canadian anti-dumping clause	28
Canadian clause a check on dumping, rather than a source of revenue	29
Effectiveness of present Canadian anti-dumping law	29
VARIOUS ASPECTS OF ANTI-DUMPING LEGISLATION IN CANADA, SOUTH AFRICA, AUSTRALIA, AND THE UNITED STATES	30

APPENDIX.

Valuation for duty and power of appraisers, collectors, and the Minister of Customs under the customs act of Canada	35
Canadian customs regulations issued in 1914	36
Specimen form of Canadian invoice	38
Anti-dumping legislation of the Union of South Africa	38
Anti-dumping legislation of Australia	39
Anti-dumping statute of the United States	42
Section 5 of the act creating the Federal Trade Commission	42
Full line forcing statute of the United States	44
Provision for countervailing duties in the United States	44
Undervaluation section of the tariff act of October 3, 1913	44
Anti-dumping paragraph adopted by the House of Representatives in 1913	45

LETTER OF TRANSMITTAL.

UNITED STATES TARIFF COMMISSION,
Washington, October 4, 1919.

COMMITTEE ON WAYS AND MEANS,
House of Representatives.

I have the honor to transmit herewith, in accordance with your request, information compiled by the United States Tariff Commission on dumping and unfair foreign competition in the United States and Canada's anti-dumping law.

Very respectfully,

THOMAS WALKER PAGE,
Acting Chairman.

INTRODUCTION.

Section 704 of the act of September 8, 1916, in part authorizes the Tariff Commission to investigate "conditions, causes, and effects relating to competition of foreign industries with those of the United States, including dumping * * *."

In 1918 the commission began an investigation into these subjects, in the course of which it sent a questionnaire relating to dumping and unfair foreign competition in the United States to many representative manufacturers, importers, exporters, and other firms and business men. Simultaneously the commission dispatched a special agent to Canada with instructions to make detailed and careful investigation of the operation of Canada's anti-dumping law. From these sources, in large measure, the facts contained in the following report were assembled.

On July 8, 1919, the Tariff Commission received a letter from Hon. Joseph W. Fordney, chairman of the Ways and Means Committee, requesting such information as the commission possessed "on the so-called Canadian anti-dumping law and its operation."

This report embodies available material, forwarded in response to that request

DUMPING AND UNFAIR FOREIGN COMPETITION IN THE UNITED STATES.

CHARACTERISTICS OF DUMPING AND CERTAIN OTHER FOREIGN COMPETITIVE PRACTICES.

DUMPING.

Dumping may be comprehensively described as the sale of imported merchandise at less than its prevailing market or wholesale price in the country of production. The definition derives particular importance from a not infrequent tendency to confuse with dumping ordinary low-price sales, price cutting and severe competition of a legitimate sort, as well as certain other trade practices which are generally considered unfairly competitive. The subject calls for clear distinctions, if many and diverse commercial complaints are to secure remedial or otherwise appropriate consideration. The anti-dumping act of Congress of September 8, 1916,[1] somewhat modifies the above definition by condemning importation as well as sale, if commonly and systematically resorted to with the purpose specified in the law. It declares unlawful—if done with the intent of destroying, injuring, or preventing the establishment of an industry or restraining or monopolizing trade or commerce in the United States—the common and systematic importation or sale of articles within the United States,

at a price substantially less than the actual market value or wholesale price of such articles at the time of exportation * * * in the principal markets of the country of of their production, or of other foreign countries to which they are commonly exported)

after adding expenses of importation and sale in the United States.

Canada's anti-dumping clause,[2] first enacted in 1904, relates to the sale rather than importation of goods, and both to casual and systematic dumping. It imposes a special dumping duty:

in the case of articles exported to Canada, of a class or kind made or produced in Canada, if the export or actual selling price to an importer in Canada be less than the fair market value of the same article when sold for home consumption in the usual and ordinary course in the country whence exported to Canada at the time of its exportation to Canada.

Similarly, the law of 1914[3] of the Union of South Africa sanctions a special dumping duty:

In the case of goods imported into the Union of a class or kind made or produced in the Union, if the export or actual selling price to an importer in the Union be less than the true current value (as defined in this act) of the same goods when sold for home consumption in the usual and ordinary course in the country from which they were exported to the Union at the time of their exportation thereto. * * *

Likewise, in the Australian act of 1906,[1] whereby dumping is expressly treated as a form of unfair competition, such unfairness is deemed established, if the imported goods

are being sold in Australia at a price which is less than gives the person importing or selling them a fair profit upon their fair foreign market value, or their fair selling

---

[1] For text of law see Appendix, p. 42.
[2] For text of law, see infra, pp. 25-6.
[3] For text of law, see Appendix, pp. 38-9.

value if sold in the country of production, together with all charges after shipment from the place whence the goods are exported directly to Australia (including customs duty).

It is apparent that these legislative declarations of the four countries mentioned are in substantial agreement as to the nature of the commercial practices the respective statutes seek to limit or prohibit.

FOREIGN GRANTS AND BOUNTIES AND COUNTERVAILING DUTIES.

For many years the tariff laws of the United States have regularly provided for the imposition of countervailing duties equal to the net amount of any grants or bounties allowed by any foreign Government in aid of the exportation of merchandise to this country.[1] The countervailing section of the act of 1894 was enacted to restrict the dumping of sugar, the production of which had been stimulated by Government bounties. Formerly, therefore, the provision for such countervailing duties was occasionally referred to as anti-dumping legislation. Reflection will show, however, that these countervailing duties possess that character in the United States only in cases where they operate against the importation or sale of articles in this country at less than their foreign market value. Indeed, what is now known as dumping has, in the main, grown from modern industrial conditions of production and distribution, without reference to direct governmental subsidies. It is a familiar development of the private promotion of the foreign trade of many industrially advanced countries. Broadly speaking, grants and bounties may or may not result in dumping. They should be regarded as aids in that direction rather than the practice itself.

FULL LINE FORCING.

The same general statement is true with reference to "full line forcing" and many other forms of unfair competition. However closely related to dumping they may be, they are not necessarily of that character. Congress, by the act of September 8, 1916,[2] provided that, in cases where merchandise is imported under any agreement that the purchaser shall be restricted, in whole or part, in using, purchasing or dealing in the articles of any other person, in addition to the regular duty, a special duty, "equal to double the amount" of the regular duty, shall be collected.

SIMULTANEOUS SACRIFICE SALES AT HOME AND ABROAD.

It logically follows that simultaneous sacrifice sales at home and abroad are not dumping unless the foreign sales are consummated on lower price levels than domestic sales. However, the Canadian and Australian statutes alike go farther and at all times reserve the right to determine the "fair" foreign market value of the articles sold.

---

[1] For text of the countervailing section of the tariff act of 1913 see Appendix, p. 44.
[2] For text of law see Appendix, p. 44.

SEVERE COMPETITION.

By the same test of definition, severe competition, however successful it may be, is not dumping. Indeed, unless featured by other elements of undue or improper advantage, such competition is not even unfair, as that term is at present customarily applied. If the restriction of keen foreign competition, when unmarked by lower foreign than domestic prices, is deemed sound economic policy, it should be proceeded with in its tariff aspects, entirely apart from the problem of dumping.

DECEPTIVE USE OF TRADE-MARKS, IMITATION OF GOODS AND ADVERTISING; FALSE LABELING; EXPLOITATION OF PATENTS; COMMERCIAL THREATS AND BRIBERY.

In the same way, unmistakable differences from dumping are evident where the deceptive use of trade-marks, deceptive imitation of goods, false labeling, exploitation of patents, deceptive advertising and commercial threats and bribery are involved. In these latter instances it is clear, without either argument or detailed analysis, that distinguishable phases of unfair competition require divergent legislative treatment from that which is indicated if the consequences of dumping are to be avoided.

UNDERVALUATION AND ADDITIONAL DUTIES.

Undervaluation occasionally appears in the technical process of making customs entry of imported merchandise, which is subject to an ad valorem duty, or to a duty based upon value. In the United States undervaluation occurs when the value of merchandise given in the entry is less than the actual foreign market value, or wholesale price, of the goods at the time of their exportation to this country. Under existing tariff laws, such undervaluation, on detection, results in the collection, over and beyond the regular duty, of an additional duty (up to 75 per cent) of 1 per cent of the total appraised value of the merchandise for each 1 per cent of appraised value in excess of the value declared in the entry. Except in cases of manifest clerical error, if the undervaluation exceeds 75 per cent of the total appraised value, the merchandise is treated as fraudulently entered, is seized and, on proof of fraud, forfeited to the Government.[1] It is plain that undervaluation, could it be commonly and systematically carried on with the intent specified in the anti-dumping act of Congress of September 8, 1916, would constitute a violation of the portion of that law which restrains the importation, no less than the sale, of goods at lower prices than those prevailing abroad. To that extent, the undervaluation paragraph is anti-dumping legislation. As a matter of fact, the tariff law of this country as construed penalizes undervaluation, whether intentional or unintentional, regardless of the accuracy and recitals of the foreign invoice. The act contemplates that the customs officer shall collect duties on the basis of

---

[1] For text of the undervaluation section, see Appendix pp. 44-5.

the foreign market value of the merchandise, at the time of its exportation to the United States, without reference to the actual price paid for such merchandise. However, as a result, the law has proven so burdensome, through the imposition of additional duties in cases of innocent and unavoidable undervaluation, that a general demand has arisen for amendment whereby, on satisfactory proof of good faith in making entry, any additional duties may be remitted or, if collected, refunded. Indeed, the Tariff Commission, itself, after careful consideration of the duties, in its Report on the Revision of the Customs Administrative Laws, has recommended this relief. Such an amendment of the law would, of course, not alter its present proper application to cases of fraudulent undervaluation, but, even taking this into account, examination of the law suggests that additional duties, as penalties for undervaluation, are not likely to prove sufficiently restrictive of dumping, since, as has been noted, the larger problem at issue is not the importation, but the sale of imported goods in the United States at less than their foreign market value. Naturally, with subsequent transactions the undervaluation section of the tariff law is not directly concerned.

THE TARIFF COMMISSION'S INQUIRY IN THE UNITED STATES.

In June, 1918, the Tariff Commission sent a letter of inquiry to the secretaries of 39 associations, including in their membership leading manufacturing establishments, importing and exporting houses, and organizations identified with business and commercial interests, such as the United States Chamber of Commerce, the Home Market Club, the American Free Trade League, the National Foreign Trade Council, and other well-known organizations. The letter requested the names and addresses of the individual members of such associations "having personal knowledge of unfair competition through the selling in the United States of articles of foreign origin at less than the fair market value when sold for home consumption in the country of origin."

In response, lists were recieved from 27 associations, with the names and addresses of 562 manufacturers, exporters, importers, and other business firms, and to these the commission mailed a questionnaire, inviting the statement of personally known instances, within 10 years, of unfair competition in articles of foreign origin, exported to the United States and sold in this country, at prices less than the actual market value or wholesale prices in the country of production, together with suggestions and opinions on legislative methods for suppressing unfair competition or dumping in the United States. In addition to this direct communication, eight associations voluntarily sent the commission's questions to their entire membership, urging, in each instance, that answers be forwarded to the secretary of the association. Five other associations, in special bulletins to members, printed the invitation and requested replies.

Two hundred and eighty-one replies were received from manufacturers and others. Of this number, 135 stated that the writers had no information of unfair foreign competition or dumping in this country; and 146 complained more or less definitely of certain forms of foreign competition encountered by them.

DUMPING AND UNFAIR FOREIGN COMPETITION. 13

INSTANCES REPORTED TO THE COMMISSION.

The examples of dumping and certain other forms of foreign competition, cited to the commission, are listed in the following table:

Reported instances of foreign competitive trade practices.	Number.	Reported instances of foreign competitive trade practices.	Number.
Dumping	23	Imitation of articles	7
Severe competition	97	Deceptive labeling	4
Threats	1	Undervaluation	8
Deceptive imitation and use of trade-marks	5	Total	146
Exploitation of patents	1		

For reference, if desired, the commission has retained in its files all answers received, but, in the interest of concise statement and illustration, it has felt impelled to summarize, rather than fully print, the typical and more relevant specifications that have reached it. In cases where the writers departed from the immediate inquiry, for example, by describing competitive conditions in foreign countries rather than in the United States, the commission has omitted the answers.

INDICATIONS OF DUMPING.

The following are condensed extracts from letters referring to dumping:

Harness leather.—There has been a great deal of Canadian harness leather sold in the United States at slight reductions in price, varying from 2 to 6 cents per pound. I have been told by Canadian buyers, at the same time that the Canadian tanners were making these reductions in the United States they were holding up prices in Canada to the consumers there. It is very hard to prove "dumping."

Harness leather.—Canadian harness leather is, in normal times, sold in the United States at less than its market value in Canada, at less than the market value of a corresponding quality of leather made in the United States, and at lower prices than the American tanner can meet, thus disposing by dumping in this country of such a percentage of their production as will enable them to maintain prices in Canada and to operate their plants at a profit.

Harness leather.—The Canadian tanneries were able to get full price at home, and they sold their surplus in the United States at a price that enabled them to get the business. They were able to bill it as off grade, or on private understanding with the buyer in a way impossible to locate definitely.

Harness leather.—As harness leather from Canada was sold in the United States before the war for less than its market value in Canada, and with the increased output of these tanneries, does it not follow that after the war the United States will be used more than ever as a dumping ground?

Sole and harness leather.—It is the general impression in the tanning trade that Canadian tanners, previous to the outbreak of the war at various times, sold harness and sole leather in large quantities in this market at lower prices than those ruling in Canada.

Black harness leather.—Large quantities of black harness leather have been sold this side of the line during the past year, and I believe at a good deal less price than the tanners were getting in Canada for it.

Calf and kid leather.—We had a short period in the fall of 1913 and in the spring of 1914 when the German tanners were relieving their market by exporting considerable stock to this country at prices lower than those ruling in Germany at the time, and this competition was keenly felt by our domestic tanners.

India kid skins.—We know of very few instances of dumping in this market. One happened seven or eight years ago in connection with India kid skins, and while this created a furore at first, it really amounted to very little.

Japanese army equipment leather.—Our representative in the East reports the sale of Japanese leather at prices that barely cover the cost of the green hide, to say nothing of the cost of manufacture. This leather has apparently been offered in good sized quantities, and it is clearly a case of dumping, very much to the detriment of American tanners.

German steel products.—The latter part of 1913 and the beginning of 1914, a representative of the "Gewerkschaft Deutscher Kaiser Hamborn" called on us and offered us steel at prices a little more than $3 per ton below the minimum prices prevailing in the United States at that time, and stated that these were only their offering prices, and if we had a contract to place, he would do better. He also admitted that the prices were much lower than were being charged to German consumers and traders. He also went so far as to say that to get money into the country they were willing to sell for export below cost.

Foreign steel bars and structural products.—During 1914 and 1915, steel bars and structural products of foreign manufacture were sold along the Atlantic seaboard at prices undoubtedly much lower than the home market prices.

Australian jams.—We would call your attention to the fact that a recent very large shipment of Australian jams has arrived in this country presumably a tender to the United States Army. When one considers the heavy import duties the Australian manufacturers have had to pay, and considers also that the tinplate used in the manufacture of these goods probably originated in this country, it would seem that the sellers of these goods must have operated at a loss. We have reason to believe that the Australian prices were much lower than these same manufacturers made in the Orient and the Straits Settlements, where all come into free competition with them.

Window glass.—The Belgian manufacturers were dumping. They were constantly selling below cost for the purpose of getting rid of a product which they could not market in Europe.

Plate glass.—There have been many times in the past history of the industry when foreign plants were selling plate glass in the United States at prices very much lower, sometimes 30 to 40 per cent lower, than they were securing in their home markets. In other words, they were dumping in the United States market.

Aniline oil.[1]—There has been a case of unfair competition on the part of Germany before the war. We understand that in 1910 a chemical company began the manufacture of aniline oil and was forced to discontinue the same by the group controlling the German manufacture of aniline oil, which dumped aniline oil in this market at a price that was approximately the manufacturing cost, with the result that this chemical company was forced to abandon the manufacture of aniline.

News print paper.—I did know of a practice in Germany, particularly by the German Verband or syndicate of news print manufacturers, who devoted one-tenth of their product for export and sold it at prices considerably below the domestic market in order to establish a price at which the Hamburg and Bremen export houses could purchase the product of manufacturers of news print in Scandinavia.

Dental supplies.—We believe that dumping has been practiced in our domestic market by Germany and perhaps by England.

Hosiery.—Under our tariff laws all hosiery at 4 marks 40 came in at one scale of duty and everything over 4 marks 40 had a higher rate of duty. Consequently the German manufacturers shipped in merchandise to this country at 4 marks 40 that they were probably getting from 5 to 6 marks for in Germany.

Hosiery.—The worst thing we see in the way of unfair foreign competition is the importation of Japanese hosiery at very much less than their value. In fact, these goods are sold at a price less than the yarn is worth in them.

Cigar bands.—There have been many times when German bands have been sold in this country at much less than the cost of manufacture in this country and undoubt-

---

[1] The Alien Property Custodian's Report (1919), pp. 30-31, makes the following statements concerning aniline oil and salycilic acid (the latter embodying an example of German pre-war dumping in this country):

"The methods under which this dumping policy was conducted and its extent may be illustrated by a few specific instances. * * * When * * * in 1910 * * * the Benzol Products Co. was organized by a group of men interested in the heavy chemical industry to manufacture anilire oil on a large scale, the German hand was immediately shown. The price of aniline oil at the time of the establishment of this company averaged 11½ cents. As soon as its manufacture was fairly underway, the German exporters commenced to cut the price. Apparently no definite prices were made by the Germans, but they adopted the simple policy of offering any customer of the new concern supplies at less than the price he was paying. For example, one of their most important customers refused an advantageous contract at 8½ cents, stating that he had assurance from the Germans that whatever price the Benzol Products Co. made would be met and bettered by them. Accordingly, the new company struggled on, conducting its operations without profit, and only because it was supported by a group of men of exceptional determination and insight was it able to survive until the war gave it an opportunity to establish its business on a firm foundation. Among other examples are the following: In 1903 there were in the United States five manufacturers of salycilic acid. In 1913 three of these had failed. * * * During the latter part of the decade referred to salycilic acid was selling in Germany at from 26½ to 30½ cents. During the same period the German houses were selling it in this country after paying a duty of 5 cents, at 25 cents, or from 6 to 10 cents below what they were getting at home."

edly less than the cost of manufacture in Germany. These bands were undoubtedly originally made for domestic consumption, but for one reason or another the goods were unsalable in Germany.

Lumber.—There have undoubtedly been times in the past when the British Columbia dealers have sold in the United States market at a lower price than they were charging their own people at home.

Jute brattice cloth and flax canvas.—Prior to 1914 jute brattice cloth sold in this country at a price less than the actual market value or wholesale price in Great Britain at the time the sale was consummated.

Burlap bags.—In the schedule relating to jute goods and bags there has always been a differential between bags and burlap, so that bags could be manufactured in this country out of burlap imported from Calcutta. Some burlap bags, however, were dumped on the Pacific coast. The maintenance of a reasonable differential in the rate on burlap in the original piece and made up bags would prevent the danger of dumping bags made in Calcutta by coolie labor.

INSTANCES OF SEVERE COMPETITION.

As illustrations of severe competition, reports of experiences in this country, among which, conceivably, some disguised examples of dumping may be included,[1] are summarized below:

Leather.—Our representative in the East reports the sale of Japanese leather at prices that barely cover the cost of the green hide, to say nothing of the cost of manufacture.

Patent leather.—After the enactment of the last tariff bill, Germany began to ship in grain-finished patent leathers made from cowhides and kid skins and these leathers were sold at a lower cost than we could produce the same article in our own country, although we were the originators of grain-finished patent leathers.

Oak sole leather.—We do know that during the early part of the year 1914 high-grade English oak sole leather bends tanned in England were exported from that country to this market in large quantities and sold here extensively at about 20 per cent less than the same kinds of leather were sold in this market.

Harness leather.—Prior to the war Canadian tanners came into the American markets and sold harness leather at considerably less than the American tanners could afford to sell it for. They sold this leather in large quantities, made from American packer hides, reexported right into the territory from which these hides originated.

Textile fabrics.—Narrow two-shuttle fancy (textile) fabrics came from Germany, mostly from the Barmen district. They were always brought in at lower prices than we could successfully compete with, even though paying 60 per cent duty. We were the pioneer manufacturers of these goods in this country.

Burlap bags.—Some years ago we had to compete with burlap bags manufactured in India, freely imported into this country, and sold at prices that were less than the same article cost us to manufacture.

Train sets.—We know of some instances where (Japanese) imported train sets are sold at a price that is not sufficient for the American manufacturer to purchase the box in which they are packed.

Steel hoops.—After the passage of the tariff act of 1913 an iron and steel manufacturer of box strapping abandoned its manufacture and became a dealer of hoops made by a German iron and steel company, obtaining them at such low prices as enabled him to undersell all other American dealers.

Horseshoe nails.—During the period from March, 1915, to June, 1916, inclusive, the imports of horseshoe nails entered at the port of Boston alone amounted to 601,075

---

[1] The following reference to oxalic acid in the Alien Property Custodian's Report (1919) p. 31, narrates a case of severe competition, in which dumping may have been practiced:
"A similar situation developed in the manufacture of oxalic acid. In 1901, when there was no American manufacture, it was sold by the Germans at 6 cents. In 1903, when the works of the American Acid & Alkali Co. were started, the price was immediately dropped to 4.7 cents, at about which figure it remained until 1907, when the American factory was shut down for a number of months. During this shutdown period the price was instantly raised to 9 cents When the factory reopened, the price was again dropped until 1908, when the company failed. It was then reorganized and in 1909 secured the imposition of a 2-cent duty on the acid, from which time up to the beginning of the war the price ran at about 7½ cents a pound. The same process was carried on in regard to bicarbonate of potash. In 1900 there was no American manufacture, and imports ran about 160,000 pounds. In 1901 American manufacture began. This succeeded so well that in 1906 imports had dropped to 45,000 pounds. At this time the American manufacturer's price was 6½ cents, while the import value was given at 4.9 cents. In the following year the Germans made a determined and successful onslaught. Their import value was lowered to 2.2 cents, with a result that instead of 45,000 pounds 310,000 pounds were imported. Accordingly, in 1908 the American manufacturer failed. The price was immediately raised to 7½ cents and remained thereabouts until the war * * *."

pounds, shipped principally from Sweden. These horseshoe nails were sold at ridiculously low prices, far below the cost of manufacture in the United States.

Chessmen.—The price that was paid by American importers for a set of foreign-made chessmen was about one-half of our net manufacturing cost, to say nothing of the overhead and the actual cost.

Twist drills.—We could not buy the high-speed steel from which German twist drills were made at the price we could buy the imported German drill complete in New York.

Hack-saw blades.—Just prior to the outbreak of the war hack-saw blades (our principal line of manufacture) of German make were sold in this market at a price very much less than our cost of manufacture.

Large machine tools.—A Pittsburgh firm purchased a large planer from a German firm at a price which we would have had to pay for castings in this country. It was delivered at the shops of the purchaser in Pittsburgh, all duties and freight paid, at about $3,000 under our price. Our machine weighed about 265,800 pounds, the German machine with boxing more.

Toy trains.—Our attention has been called to a Japanese toy train retailing in this country at 15 cents. We would have to charge such a price for a similar article that the retailer would have to get 75 cents.

Cigar bands.—There have been many times when German cigar bands have been sold in this country at much less than the cost of manufacture in this country.

Calendars.—It is a matter of general knowledge in the printing and lithographing trade that all color work, such as calendars, etc., made in Germany in the past 10 years, have come into this country at a less price than would have been the cost of production here.

Lithography.—Any and all items in the lithographic industry have always (even with duties against them) been marketed at prices which we could never manufacture and compete against.

Labels.—This year a certain Pacific coast lighographer quoted $1.10 per thousand on several million sardine labels. The Japanese price for the same goods was 51 cents per thousand, delivered in California.

Bent-wood chairs.—Chairs manufactured in Austria and known as bent-wood chairs have been disposed of in this country at considerably less than we can produce them for. We also learned on good authority that for chairs we manufacture, which cost us $18 per dozen, the foreigner is able to place in New York finished, knocked down, at $8, including freight and duty.

Veneers and plywood.—During 1913 and the early part of 1914 we had competition in veneers and plywood, as we understand, made in Russia and placed on sale in this country at a cost about equalling the labor it took in this country to produce it, leaving nothing for material.

CHARGES OF DECEPTIVE IMITATION OF GOODS; FALSE LABELING; AND DECEPTIVE USE OF TRADE-MARKS.

Samples of representative statements made in the letters to the commission concerning deceptive imitation of goods, false labeling and deceptive use of trade-marks are here abbreviated:

Button machines and buttons.—During the year 1907, Hugo E. Brenner of Bremen, Germany, obtained from us on a contract, sample machines, patterns and blue prints complete, with which he could make additional machines in Germany for the manufacture of buttons and fasteners identically the same as our product. He in return was to sell his product in Europe only, we to get a royalty on all he manufactured. He kept his agreement up to the early part of 1914 and had a nice business abroad, when he stopped paying us royalties and commenced exporting his product to the United States, stating he could sell cheaper f. o. b. New York than it cost us to manufacture the product. We started suit against him and obtained a judgment in the New York courts, but to date have not been able to collect.

Grass rugs.—We have come directly into competition with Japanese goods which are made up as imitations of our own product. Absolute copies are made of exclusive designs owned by us, the product is imitated exactly as to appearance, and these rugs are marketed and advertised in this country as "grass rugs," which is the name under which the domestic product gained an enviable reputation, whereas in fact they are made of rice straw. This copying of domestic patterns is very common on Japanese goods. A letter on our desk this morning from one of our San Francisco selling agents says: "I was also told this morning that three American importers in San Francisco are selling considerable grass rugs from Japan particularly copies of our patterns."

DUMPING AND UNFAIR FOREIGN COMPETITION. 17

Knit goods underwear.—The American trade-mark label and pasteboard box container of "pioneer mesh" underwear of a New York State knitting company were imitated and reproduced by a Japanese concern. The Japanese box and label were exact imitations of the American in its illustrative cut and the different forms of printing used.

Lead pencils.—We wish to call your attention to the misuse of the name or mark "Duma" as used in connection with a pencil, manufactured by this company for many years (sample of which we enclose herewith), and sold very extensively in the Philippine markets. Note the poor finish and quality of the enclosed Japanese sample and the improper centering of the lead, also that our exact number, 1005, is made use of besides the adoption of the word "Duma" as used by us. The shape and color are almost identical. The article above described is sold in the Philippine markets and it would naturally follow that the regulations governing the imports at Manila should be the same as the regulations governing the imports coming into the United States.

These Japanese pencils are very much inferior in quality and are sold in the same markets as we sell the American article and in competition therewith. Dealers because of their similarity believe them to be American goods and when the poor quality is discovered, it naturally reflects discredit upon the American manufacturer's goods, and not only this, but the Japanese articles, because of their inferiority are sold for much less than the American article can be manufactured for.

Then again it is the practice of the Japanese who export pencils to the United States and the Philippine markets to guarantee these articles to be first quality "drawing" pencils, although they are of extremely poor quality and workmanship and they are entered at a minimum value. They sell them for about $1.05 whereas the pencil manufacturers of this country can not consistently presume to guarantee a pencil for drawing purposes which will sell for less than about $2.50. Among the trade and in the mind of the consumer, a pencil for drawing purposes is standardized and is looked upon as a superior article, possessing suitable quality and grading requisites to warrant its designation as such. Here in the case of the Japanese article the quality, proper grading and workmanship are all lacking and the consuming public, because of the misuse of descriptive wording, is deceived.

COMPLAINTS OF UNDERVALUATION.

The most pertinent intimations of undervaluation in the letters received by the commission may be abridged as follows:

Hosiery.—It is a fact that during the last 10 years and previous, importations of full fashioned hosiery have been made at values below those of our product, and we have assumed that undervaluations have occurred. This view, we think, has generally been accepted by the trade.

French balbriggan underwear.—The importers of this class of merchandise were enabled to defeat, to a great extent, the principle of ad valorem tariff rates by a special regulation of their purchases in the following manner: The manufacturer in France would show a line of samples covering values of about 10 francs for the cheaper grade and proportionate advances for the better grade. Orders would be accepted for the cheaper grades, provided the customer would also purchase a certain quantity of the better grades. This method secured for the importer the lowest rates of duty and he was, thereby, enabled to defeat the purpose of the tariff rate which had been designed to protect manufacturers of the cheaper classes of balbriggan underwear.

Steel dental instruments.—There has been undervaluation of steel dental instruments from Germany.

Jewelry.—Several jewelers were told by German importers in New York when the Payne-Aldrich bill was passed, with practically 85 per cent duty, that German goods would be brought into the United States and sold in competition regardless of the duty, and quantities of German goods were brought into America with 85 per cent duty staring them in the face, and undervaluation was the chief lever used.

Pottery.—As a result of a governmental investigation under the direction of the Secretary of the Treasury in the industry with which I am connected, it was developed that cups and saucers protected by a tariff rate of duty of 55 and 60 per cent were being imported from Holland and Germany and were undervalued fully 60 per cent.

141566—19——3

COMMENTS ON RESULTS OF THE COMMISSION'S INQUIRY.

FAIR AND UNFAIR COMPETITIVE METHODS TO BE DISTINGUISHED.

These net results of the commission's request for detailed information, though the instances cited are frequently lacking in certainty, and, in some respects, are unexpectedly few in number, exemplify the definitions given at the outset of this report. The answers, as already noted, evidence a tendency to complain indiscriminately, not only of these methods condemned everywhere as unfair, but also of every form of successful foreign competition. The latter attitude, if given legal sanction, would affect American business usages in the promotion of foreign trade and would invite retaliation by other countries. Ordinary price cutting and underselling are so universal, both in domestic and foreign fields, that it is taken for granted that restrictions are contemplated only when their practice is accompanied by unfair circumstances or by unfortunate public consequences.

DIFFICULTY OF PROVING DUMPING.

With particular reference to the inconclusive character of some of the recitals of dumping, it must be borne in mind that, in the absence of governmental machinery devoted to its detection, conclusive proof of dumping is difficult to obtain. Until 1916 no statute of the United States had declared the practice unlawful and, even since that time, no governmental agency other than the Department of Justice has been particularly interested in its prevention. In the absence of large investigating powers the task of an individual who seeks to convert suspicious circumstances into proof, one element of which must be found abroad, is usually of extreme difficulty. This observation is supported by the experience of Canada. There, previous to 1904, when the antidumping clause was enacted, while complaints of dumping were common, the evidence was unsatisfactory and scattered. The Canadian law armed customs administrative agents of the Dominion with powers of inspection both at ports of entry, and, for a first time (on penalty of exclusion of merchandise for denial of access to original books), in the countries of exportation. In consequence, many instances of attempted dumping in Canada were discovered.

In a letter to the Tariff Commission, the Tanners' Council of the United States comments as follows on the situation, under existing law in this country:

It has recently been alleged that certain Canadian tanners are selling leather to American manufacturers at less than the fair market price prevailing in Canada, to the detriment of our domestic tanning industry. * * * At present a manufacturer who is injured because his former customers are importing dumped goods from abroad would hesitate to take his case to the courts unless he was very sure of his ground, and even then the expense, delay, and uncertainty of litigation would be likely to restrain him. Furthermore, the wording of the present antidumping clause makes it very difficult for either the Government in a criminal prosecution or for an aggrieved manufacturer in a civil suit to obtain a verdict. The difficulty of proving that dumping is practiced with the intent of destroying a United States industry or of monopolizing the trade in a certain article would have a decidedly deterrent effect on both criminal prosecutions and civil suits. A manufacturer would also have difficulty in recovering in a civil suit because of the necessity of proving the common and systematic importation of dumped goods and because of the ambiguity of the phrase "substantially less" used in connection with the fair market value of dumped goods in the country of exportation.

EXPLANATION OF DUMPING PRACTICES.

In the light of the evidence, the reality of the attempts, at least from time to time, to dump goods in this country will hardly be doubted. Canada's experience is at hand, and the recent war tended to uncover the extent to which German business firms formerly promoted dumping practices in this country. In this connection, the United States Alien Property Custodian [1] gives, in part, the following account of the growth of the German dye industry:

* * * The improvements in processes brought about by research laid heavy emphasis on the value of quantity production. Quantity production, carried on by competing houses, led to overproduction. Overproduction led to a determined effort to establish and maintain a large export trade. The natural advantages of the German industry, as compared to the industry in other countries, prevented serious competition in Germany itself. The Government's tariff and other policies enabled home prices to be kept up. It was then evidently to the advantage of any manufacturer to produce far more than he could sell in the home market, even if his export trade had to be carried on at a loss, when by doing so he could use a process so economical that his profits on home trade would be largely increased. Accordingly, German dyestuffs began to appear in every country at prices which domestic manufacturers could not meet. * * *

Indeed, as the preceding quotation tends to establish, dumping is a not unnatural development of the growth of the foreign trade of industrially advanced countries. For one thing, the existence of surplus stock, particularly in periods of business depression, when the home market is indifferent or supplied, invites at least spasmodic dumping in foreign fields. For years it has been undisputed that certain American manufacturers have dumped a portion of their product abroad. Manufacturers themselves have frequently claimed that in large scale operations and with mass production, economies may be effected; and that these result in cheaper sales, both domestic and foreign, than would otherwise be possible when the manufacturer is assured of the regular absorption abroad of surplus stocks at somewhat lower prices than at home.[2] Such dumping, of course, tends to become permanent, and indulgence in the usage, it would appear plain, assesses against the consumers who reside in the country of production the expense of any unremunerative attempts to capture foreign markets. We find, however, in the real or anticipated effects of "economic penetration" on the established industries in foreign countries where the dumping occurs, the explanation of the enactment of antidumping legislation. Not only is there frequent complaint in such countries that domestic production is hampered or prevented, but it is even pointed out that, with production controlled, there is no assurance that the dumped prices will not eventually be arbitrarily raised even to excessive levels.

---

[1] Report of the Alien Property Custodian (1919), p. 30.
[2] "The ability of the foreigner to dump his goods in this country, not only without losing by the process, but actually increasing his profits thereby, is brought out by the figures supplied by a British firm. Last year they produced 114,000 tons, the cost per ton in the conditions then prevalent being £4 15s. Selling this at an average price of £5 per ton, their profit was £28,500. But if their works had been employed to their full capacity, namely, 152,000 tons, the cost per ton would have been reduced to £4 10s. This extra production of 38,000 tons could have been sold at cost price, and yet, owing to the all-round reduction upon cost of production, their profit would have become £57,000. Thus, it will be seen that they could have sold this 38,000 tons at considerably below cost, and still have increased their profits had there been any market in which they had been able to dispose of it.

"In view of these conditions, it is, in our opinion, impossible to maintain that dumping is merely a temporary expedient, unprofitable to the countries which practice it, and, therefore, certain to be abandoned. In fact, the evidence indicates that dumping is part of an organized policy. The evidence further suggests that just as foreign competition, commencing at the lower stages of production has, as we have shown, gradually extended, so foreign countries must inevitably find it profitable to dump in branch after branch of the more finished manufactures as their productive power increases." "The Iron and Steel Trades," vol. 1, 65-6: Report of The (Chamberlain) Tariff Commission (London, 1904).

The first apparent consequence of dumping in the country in which goods are sold at lower prices than those prevailing in the country of exportation is a gain, in the form of reduced cost of articles, to consumers, or, in the case of raw or semimanufactured materials, to manufacturers. An illustration of this effect is commonly regarded as having been furnished by the confectionery and jam industries of Great Britain during the well-known period when beet sugar was being dumped in England from Europe.[1] Likewise, at one time the revival of the British tin plate industry was largely credited to the dumping of cheap steel in the British Islands.[2] Therefore, in so far as the dumped merchandise is not made or produced in the country of sale, the transaction is one to which the latter country is not ordinarily disposed to object. The problem arises from the competitive pressure of these reduced prices when the dumped goods are similar to those domestically produced. Dumping, from this standpoint, is a form of competition having extreme, and unpredictable manifestations. As such, it departs, in a measure, from the ordinary conditions of domestic supply and demand and introduces elements which are met, if at all, with apprehension and difficulty. The dumping of goods may have the effect of forcing domestic manufacturers to sell their entire output at a small margin of profit, or even at a loss. Moreover, even the quotation of dumping prices, though no sales in fact be made, may occasionally result in compelling merchants with established trade to cut their prices in order to hold their business against threats of dumping competition.

INTENT AS AN ELEMENT IN DUMPING.

It should also be observed that economic conditions are more significant in the development of dumping practices than is any particular intent. In conducting private industry the prevailing motive is profit. Ordinarily, therefore, it must be extremely difficult to establish, as an essential element in the offense, a separate and destructive purpose, as specified in the congressional act of 1916. In dumping, the intent to injure, destroy, or prevent the establishment of an industry, or to restrain or monopolize trade or commerce in the United States, is not necessarily present. Certainly, when the practice is resorted to, motives other than those enumerated may, and, at times, do exist. Among such incentives we may expect the desire, through the aid rendered by the consumption of surplus stocks abroad, to secure and sustain full capacity production; the retention, in part thereby, of established organization and more

---

[1] "These dumped importations of refined Continental sugar were for a period advantageous to manufacturing confectioners by providing them with sugar at artificially low prices. But these low prices were of a temporary character only and the result of conditions incompatible with the permanent expansion of the confectionery industry." "Sugar and Confectionery," vol. 7, 4: Report of The (Chamberlain) Tariff Commission (London, 1907).

[2] See statements of witnesses: "The Iron and Steel Trades," vol. 1, Report of The (Chamberlain) Tariff Commission, e. g. 1145, 1155.
"* * * The dumping that is unfair competition from the point of view of one set of producers—themselves often as 'unfair' in their own competition—may be a boon and a blessing to another set. A good many years ago the British tinplate trade was in a depressed state as a result of the prohibitive McKinley tariff on their product in the United States. During the year of forewarning, the trade made immense profits, American canners buying all they could in advance: then the trade fell on hard times. But soon it came about that German producers of steel were dumping on the British market at prices much below those previously current, and that cheap steel was the salvation of the tinplate trade. An 'anti-dumping' duty would have prevented the salvation, in the interests of the British producers of steel, though in point of fact the saving of the tinplate trade meant the saving of their own future market." "The New Tariffism," J. M. Robertson, M. P. (London, 1918) p. 57.

effective mechanical operations; and the reduction, through these various factors, of fixed and overhead charges and of direct costs of production per unit of product.

CANADA'S ANTI-DUMPING LAW.

THE TARIFF COMMISSION'S INVESTIGATION IN CANADA.

The operation of Canada's anti-dumping law was investigated by the Tariff Commission in 1918. In that year, the commission sent a representative to Canada for this special purpose, and the commission desires to record its indebtedness for marked courtesies, extended to it and its agent, throughout the investigation, by the officials of the Dominion Government. Every official facility for proceeding with the inquiry was promptly and freely accorded. The commission's representative, as a result of his examination, reported that the specific data in the official files clearly establish the fact that dumping has been attempted in Canada in a large number of instances, and in connection with many manufactured articles and industries.

The inquiry was not limited to the review of official records. Canadian manufacturers and importers also were interviewed, and their views on the operation of the anti-dumping legislation, and its effects upon Canadian industries and trade, were sought and obtained. Certain expressions of responsible spokesmen for these groups are included hereafter in this report.

CANADA'S ORIGINAL ANTI-DUMPING PROVISION, ENACTED IN 1904.

Canada's original anti-dumping clause was formally introduced in the House of Commons on June 28, 1904, as an amendment to the customs tariff act of 1897. As enacted into law on August 10, 1904, it provided:[1]

Whenever it appears to the satisfaction of the minister of customs, or of any officer of customs authorized to collect customs duties, that the export price or the actual selling price to the importer in Canada of any imported dutiable article, of a class or kind made or produced in Canada, is less than the fair market value thereof, as determined according to the basis of value for duty provided in the *Customs Act* in respect of imported goods subject to an ad valorem duty, such article shall, in addition to the duty otherwise established, be subject to a special duty of customs equal to the difference between such fair market value and such selling price: Provided, however, That the special customs duty on any article shall not exceed one-half of the customs duty otherwise established in respect of the article, except in regard to the articles mentioned in items 224, 226, 228, and 231 in schedule A to the *Customs Tariff*, 1897, the special duty of customs on which shall not exceed 15 per cent ad valorem, nor more than the difference between the selling price and the fair market value of the article.

2. The expression "export price" or "selling price" in this section shall be held to mean and include the exporter's price for the goods, exclusive of all charges thereon after their shipment from the place whence exported directly to Canada.

3. This section shall apply to imported round rolled wire rods not over three-eighths of an inch in diameter, notwithstanding that such rods are on the customs free list: Provided, however, That the special duty of customs on such wire rods shall not exceed 15 per cent ad valorem.

4. If at any time it appears to the satisfaction of the Governor in Council on a report from the Minister of Customs that the payment of the special duty by this section provided for is being evaded by the shipment of goods on consignment without sale prior to such shipment, the Governor in Council may in any case or class of cases

---

[1] Statutes of Canada (1904), 4 Edw. VII, ch. 11, sec. 19.

authorize such action as is deemed necessary to collect on such goods or any of them the same special duty as if the goods had been sold to an importer in Canada prior to their shipment to Canada.

5. If the full amount of any special duty of customs is not paid on goods imported, the customs entry thereof shall be amended and the deficiency paid upon the demand of the collector of customs.

6. The Minister of Customs may make such regulations as are deemed necessary for carrying out the provisions of this section and for the enforcement thereof.

7. Such regulations may provide for the temporary exemption from special duty of any article or class of articles, when it is established to the satisfaction of the Minister of Customs that such articles are not made in Canada in substantial quantities and offered for sale to all purchasers on equal terms.

8. Such regulations may also provide for the exemption from special duty of any article whereon the duty in schedule A is equal to 50 per cent ad valorem or upwards, or when the difference between the fair market value of the goods and the selling price thereof to the importer as aforesaid amounts only to a small percentage of their fair market value.

9. This section shall not apply to goods of a class subject to excise duty in Canada.

REASONS ASSIGNED FOR CANADA'S LEGISLATION OF 1904.

The adoption of the above Canadian clause is perhaps best explained in the language of Hon. W. S. Fielding, minister of finance, in outlining the original legislation in his budget speech of June 7, 1904. In the course of that speech Mr. Fielding said:[1]

We find to-day that the high tariff countries have adopted that method of trade which has now come to be known as slaughtering, or perhaps the word more frequently used is dumping; that is to say, that the trust or combine, having obtained command and control of its own market and finding that it will have a surplus of goods, sets out to obtain command of a neighboring market, and for the purpose of obtaining control of a neighboring market will put aside all reasonable considerations with regard to the cost or fair price of the goods; the only principle recognized is that the goods must be sold and the market obtained. I quite realize that what I may call the extreme free trader, that is, the theoretical free trader, if there be such a man, who attaches more importance to a theory than to the practical things of this life may ask: "Why should we care about that; do we not get the benefit of cheap goods?" Well, if we could be guaranteed for ever or for a long period that we would obtain cheap goods under that system, the question would be a very fair one. If these trusts and combines in the high tariff countries would come under obligations, with sufficient bonds, to supply us with these goods at the lowest prices for the next 50 years, it would probably be the part of wisdom for us to close up some of our industries and turn the energies of our people to other branches. But surely none of us imagine that when these high tariff trusts and combines send goods into Canada at sacrifice prices they do it for any benevolent purpose. They are not worrying about the good of the people of Canada. They send the goods here with the hope and the expectation that they will crush out the native Canadian industries. And with the Canadian industry crushed out, what would happen? The end of cheapness would come, and the beginning of dearness would be at hand. Artificial cheapness obtained to-day under such conditions, at the expense of dearness at a very near day in the future, is not a system of which we could approve or which any of us on either side of the House could encourage. This dumping, then, is an evil and we propose to deal with it. Perhaps it would not be too much to say that 90 per cent of the complaints that are made to us by our manufacturers are not that the tariff is too low, speaking generally, but that this dumping and slaughtering condition exists, and that the tariff under such conditions fails to give them the protection they would desire. Well, if 90 per cent of these grievances result from dumping, we shall be prepared to deal with it to-day. We think it is in the interest of legitimate trade that this question should be dealt with. It is not the first time that Canada has set an example in matters of this kind and possibly the step we are about to take will be followed by other countries. Our friends on the other side of the House will recognize this dumping evil as fully as and perhaps more fully than even gentlemen on this side on the House. We differ from them as to the manner in which it should be dealt with. Their remedy is a general increase of the tariff all along the line. Perhaps they would not go quite so far as to increase all duties, but that is the principle they suggest. A high tariff is their remedy

---

[1] Debates of the House of Commons, Dominion of Canada, sess. 1904, Vol. III, 4364-7.

for this evil. We object to that because we think it is unscientific. The dumping condition is not a permanent condition, it is a temporary condition, and therefore it needs only a temporary remedy that can be applied whenever the necessity for it arises.

We proposed, therefore, to impose a special duty upon dumped goods. That special duty, subject to a limitation which I will mention, will be the difference between the price at which the goods are sold, the sacrifice price, and the fair market value of those goods as established under the customs law of the country. But this is subject to a qualification, they are subject to a limitation. If an article is sold at a lower price in Canada than it is sold in the country of production, then that will be the evidence of dumping, and the difference between the fair market value in the country of production and the price at which it is sold—or if honorable gentlemen prefer, dumped—that difference shall constitute the special duty, within the limitations. As regards certain articles upon which our duties are low and upon which we grant protection in the form of bounties as well as in the form of duties, as respects certain of these items in the iron schedule chiefly, the limitation shall be 15 per cent ad valorem; that is to say, that special duty shall be the difference between the fair price and the dumping price, provided it shall not exceed 15 per cent ad valorem. The additional duty over and above the present duty I call the special duty, and it is so called in our resolutions. Then in case of other articles, the limit is 50 per cent of the present duty. It is a duty over and above the existing duty, and it is limited by these two conditions: In one case, or in a few cases of like character, the limitation is that it shall not exceed 15 per cent, and in the other case it shall not exceed one-half of the duty. * * *

* * * There is a provision in the existing law that where there is an undervaluation you can levy duty upon the true valuation. Suppose, for illustration, that an article of which the true value is $100 is entered at $80, you can impose the duty on the whole $100. You get, therefore, an extra duty in that case, if you care to look at it in that way, to the extent of the rate of duty on the difference in value. In what we propose, you get the whole difference itself. If the article is sold at $80 and if the fair market value is $100, under the law as it stands to-day you get your duty of say, 30 per cent on that extra $20. Under what we now propose you not only get the duty on the full $100 but an extra duty, which means the $20 itself, subject to the limitation that it shall not be greater than one-half of the duty. Thus, if the duty is 30 per cent, the extra duty, or the special duty as I describe it, can not exceed 15 per cent, and the whole duty could not exceed 45 per cent. The principle is that we will impose as a special duty the difference between the true value and the unfair value. But we put a limitation on that, as limitations are put upon all forms of taxation. Our information is that the average of dumping in Canada represents about 15 per cent. There are some cases in which the dumping may be more and some in which it may be less; but from the best information we can obtain we think that the dumping averages a cut price, an unfair price, an illegitimate price, to the extent of about 15 per cent. With the limitation that we are putting on, it is a special duty corresponding with what we believe to be the average amount of dumping. I may say there is also a special clause with regard to a possible evasion of the provision by the consignee of the goods. * * *

Later, on June 28, 1904, discussing some proposed changes in the tariff resolutions, Mr. Fielding added: [1]

* * * In what is commonly called the dumping clause, it is proposed to insert words which will empower the Minister of Customs in his regulations to make a temporary exemption as respects the operation of that clause in cases where the goods referred to are not manufactured in Canada in large quantity and in open competition. It would be possible that an article might be made in Canada to a very small extent, or it would perhaps be in the hands of some one producer and not open to the trade. It is felt that if such a condition should arise it might not be a proper case for the application of the dumping clause. The amendment will therefore provide that the Minister of Customs may, in his regulations, temporarily exempt from the operation of the special duty—that is the technical phrase I use, or the dumping clause—articles of a class where the minister is satisfied that the articles are not made in Canada in a substantially large quantity and open to sale on even terms to all applicants. Though an article may be made in Canada ordinarily exceptional circumstances may arise, such as a strike, which would stop the manufacture in Canada and in that case the Minister of Customs ought to have some discretion to meet a condition that might arise. That is the object of the amendment. * * *

---

[1] Debates of the House of Commons, Dominion of Canada, session 1904, Vol. III, 5737-8.

CANADIAN TARIFF HEARINGS IN 1905-6.

Following the adoption of the anti-dumping clause of 1904, and prior to the tariff revision in Canada in 1907, the operation of the clause was considered, with other tariff matters, at a series of hearings held in the years 1905-6 in the principal manufacturing and agricultural centers of the various Provinces of the Dominion by the Canadian ministers of finance, customs, and internal revenue. These hearings ended in February, 1906, and thereafter the Government decided to offer amendments to the anti-dumping clause as originally enacted.

The record of these tariff sessions, though preserved, has not been officially printed, on which account it is not practicable to incorporate here customary and authoritative references. Nevertheless, because of its bearing on the history of Canada's legislation, the testimony thus taken is here, in part, briefly abstracted.

ADMINISTRATION OF THE ANTI-DUMPING CLAUSE OF 1904.

During the hearings, in reply to a stove manufacturer, who asserted that the dumping clause had not been applied to stoves imported from the United States, Minister Fielding said:

> You know the conditions. You have to prove that the selling price here is not the selling price for American consumption. If the price for Canada is the same as that which the goods are sold at for consumption in the United States, there is no dumping; it is a matter of price. You claim this is not the natural price, but what you call an overproduction price, and that they would not sell for the same price in the United States. * * * If you could satisfy us that there was an evasion, we would send men to find out the facts.

On another occasion, Minister Fielding further commented, as follows, on the administration of the law:

> The Customs Department requires the importer to show on his invoices two columns; that is to say, the price in the market for home consumption in the United States and the price at which these goods have been purchased. Therefore, if that statement is honestly made the evidence is before the Customs Department; if that is not honestly made, then there is a fraud.

THE 1904 CLAUSE OPPOSED IN 1905-6 BY FARMERS AND IMPORTERS.

At these tariff hearings, held in agricultural centers, the anti-dumping clause of 1904 was opposed by farmers, as having led to increases to the cost to western immigrant farmers of lumber, stoves, hardware, and agricultural implements needed in pioneer farming and development. The clause was also opposed by groups of importers connected with department stores and engaged in hardware and other lines of business. The Canadian Wholesale Hardware Association asked for the repeal of the law, assigning as reasons that the legislation was impossible of equitable application; an encouragement to fraud; an injustice to honest importers; and an unwarranted restriction of freedom to purchase; also, that it tended to take the trade in affected lines from Canadian wholesale merchants and give it to former competitors; and that, with resultant serious loss on contracts, it unduly enhanced the laid-down cost of such commodities as Canadian manufacturers, when crowded with business, were unable to supply.

The Wholesale Druggists of Canada registered the following protest against the operation of the clause:

We would point out that portions of this clause prevent the importer from making a good bargain upon articles that are adequately protected by a duty.

A representative of a large importing house expressed the opinion that prices to Canadian trade, before the clause was in force, were the same as to other foreign trade, and were not lower than fair values. He further stated that the operation of the dumping clause, as a rule, injured the consumer and benefited no one, except American manufacturers, who generally raised their prices correspondingly.

THE 1904 CLAUSE INDORSED IN 1905-6 BY MANUFACTURING INDUSTRIES.

On the other hand, at the hearing, the manufacturing interests of Canada strongly indorsed the anti-dumping clause. While favoring amendment and more thorough enforcement, all urged the retention of the law. Illustrative of their general attitude was the following statement, addressed to Hon. William Patterson, Minister of Customs, by more than 40 of the principal iron and steel manufacturers of the Dominion:

We heartily approve of the principle embodied in the tariff legislation of 1904, but we are of the opinion that steps should be taken by the Government to give more practical effect to the legislation. The checking branch of the Customs Department of Ottawa doubtless does what is possible to insure uniformity of values at the different ports, and we recognize that an important aid to this end was given by the requirement of duplicate invoices with all entries—the second copy going to the Department of Customs at Ottawa for checking purposes. We believe, however, that yet greater safeguards against evasion of the revenue laws can be provided, particularly by the appointment of a staff of competent inspecting appraisers. The subject is not a new one. It has been pressed upon the attention of the Government on more than one occasion, and we are convinced that great good would result both to the revenue and to the trade of the country by the adoption of this suggestion. The expense of such a staff would be very trifling and not comparable with the increase in revenue likely to be provided by this work, and we can conceive of no step better calculated to bring about uniformity of values and ratings the country over.

Another suggestion we have to offer is that one or more officers of the Customs Department be appointed, with residence in Great Britain, for the purpose of investigating values, origin of goods, etc. Such officers could also render useful service in instructing British exporters regarding our customs laws and regulations. We have learned with pleasure of the action of the Minister of Customs in placing an adequate staff of officers in the principal cities of the United States to assist in carrying out the work of his department, and we trust that a similar step will be taken as regards Great Britain. The only other recommendation we desire to make tending the special Anti-Dumping Clause is in regard to the exemption that has been made regarding its operation in cases where the difference between the value for duty and the selling price does not exceed 5 per cent.

We think that this should be abolished, as such exemption weakens the principle of the legislation by permitting a certain degree of slaughtering besides introducing a complicated regulation.

CANADA'S ANTI-DUMPING CLAUSE, AS AMENDED IN 1907, AND NOW IN FORCE.

On April 12, 1907, Canada revised its tariff, including the anti-dumping clause of 1904. As amended, and now in force, that clause reads:[1]

6. In the case of articles exported to Canada of a class or kind made or produced in Canada, if the export or actual selling price to an importer in Canada is less than the fair market value of the same article when sold for home consumption in the

---

[1] Statutes of Canada 1907, 6-7 Edw. VII, Vol. I-II, p. 134.

usual and ordinary course in the country whence exported to Canada at the time of its exportation to Canada, there shall, in addition to the duties otherwise established, be levied, collected, and paid on such article, on its importation into Canada, a special duty (or dumping duty) equal to the difference between the said selling price of the article for export and the said fair market value thereof for home consumption; and such special duty (or dumping duty) shall be levied, collected, and paid on such article, although it is not otherwise dutiable.

Provided that the said special duty shall not exceed 15 per cent ad valorem in any case;

Provided also that the following goods shall be exempt from such special duty, viz:
 (a) Goods whereon the duties otherwise established are equal to 50 per cent ad valorem;
 (b) Goods of a class subject to excise duty in Canada;
 (c) Sugar refined in the United Kingdom;
 (d) Binder twine or twine for harvest binders manufactured from New Zealand hemp, istle, or tampico fiber, sisal grass, or sunn, or a mixture of any two or more of them, of single ply and measuring not exceeding 600 feet to the pound.

Provided further that excise duties shall be disregarded in estimating the market value of goods for the purposes of special duty when the goods are entitled to entry under the British Preferential Tariff.

2. "Export price" or "selling price" in this section shall be held to mean and include the exporter's price for the goods, exclusive of all charges thereon after their shipment from the place whence exported directly to Canada.

3. If at any time it appears to the satisfaction of the Governor in Council, on a report from the Minister of Customs, that the payment of the special duty by this section provided for is being evaded by the shipment of goods on consignment without sale prior to such shipment, the Governor in Council may in any case or class of cases authorize such action as is deemed necessary to collect on such goods or any of them the same special duty as if the goods had been sold to an importer in Canada prior to their shipment to Canada.

4. If the full amount of any special duty of Customs is not paid on goods imported, the Customs entry thereof shall be amended and the deficiency paid upon the demand of the collector of customs.

5. The Minister of Customs may make such regulations as are deemed necessary for carrying out the provisions of this section and for the enforcement thereof.

6. Such regulations may provide for the temporary exemption from special duty of any article or class of articles when it is established to the satisfaction of the Minister of Customs that such articles are not made or sold in Canada in substantial quantities and offered for sale to all purchasers on equal terms under like conditions, having regard to the custom and usage of trade.

7. Such regulations may also provide for the exemption from special duty of any article when the difference between the fair market value and the selling price thereof to the importer as aforesaid amounts only to a small percentage of its fair market value.

AMENDMENTS OF 1907.

By the amendments of 1907 certain goods are specifically exempted from the application of the dumping duty; in estimating market value, excise duties on goods entitled to entry under the British preferential tariff are to be disregarded; the circumstances under which the minister of customs may allow temporary exemptions from that duty are more carefully defined; the dumping duty, when applied, is limited to 15 per cent ad valorem, and reference to one-half the ordinary duty, previously fixed as a maximum in some instances, is omitted; and the clause, which formerly affected dutiable merchandise only, is extended to apply to goods on the free list as well.

Prior to the enactment of the customs tariff, Minister Fielding, in his budget speech of November 29, 1906, discussed some of the proposed amendments as follows:[1]

We introduced a couple of years ago a rather novel piece of legislation known as the dumping clause. There was some friction at the time, as there always will be in the introduction of any new feature of tariff legislation, but the friction has pretty

---

[1] Debates of House of Commons, Dominion of Canada, session 1906–7, vol. 1, p. 304.

well passed away, and it will be generally admitted that this clause has on the whole served its purpose very well. We propose to continue the dumping clause and enlarge it in this respect. Hitherto it has applied only to dutiable goods. We propose to strike out the restriction and make it apply to imports whether dutiable or free. The special duty, or the dumping duty, as it is familiarly termed—and, by the way, the word has now been sufficiently naturalized for us to import it into the tariff, and we are going to honor it by placing it there—was the difference in value between the true value and what for convience I may call the false value of the goods—at all events, the cut value, but subject to this limitation, that the difference should not exceed one-half of the ordinary duties. We propose to change that slightly so that hereafter it will read that the dumping or special duty shall be the difference in value as before, provided it does not in any case exceed 15 per cent. Thus, in the case of an article on the free list, if the dumping principle be applied, the duty to be charged would be the difference in value—the improper difference as we deem it—not, however, to exceed 15 per cent.

Subsequently, on January 10, 1907, Mr. Fielding commented on the suggested application of the law to free as well as dutiable goods, in these words:[1]

The object of the dumping duty has been accepted on both sides, though of course there are differences of opinion as to the manner of its application. But the principle has been accepted that when foreign articles are sold below a fair reasonable price, with the sole object of crushing out some home industry, then the dumping duty should be applied. If that principle be a sound one as applied to articles on the dutiable list, it is still more applicable to articles on the free list, because in the former case the home manufacturer has some protection while in the other he has none at all. Once we accept the principle of the dumping duty, it must be admitted that it ought apply to free goods in cases where similar goods are made in Canada and the prices of the foreign articles are cut down for the express purpose of crushing out some Canadian industry.

The same day the purpose of the provision specifically exempting from the dumping duty, among other things, "binder twine or twine for harvest binders" was thus explained:[2]

Mr. FIELDING. * * * At first glance that may seem to be something that should not be exempt. But I would invite a moment's consideration of one point involved. Binder twine is one of the articles which, to some extent, we are now exporting to the United States. Binder twine of certain classes is now admitted into the United States free and our manufacturers are exporting to that country.

* * * * * * *

Mr. PATTERSON. There is this special reason, that there is an export trade from the United States of $363,000. The provision in the American tariff which makes this article free has another provision attached to it, that the articles mentioned in the paragraph, if imported from a country which lays an import duty on raw articles imported from the United States, shall be subject to a duty of one-half of 1 per [*sic*] cent per pound. Now we admit it free, but if the twine was coming in under the price at which it is sold there and were made subject to the special exemption, it would come under this provision. A special exception would make it subject to the dumping duty, which the United States authorities would rule was the imposition of a duty, and therefore their duty would apply against Canadian manufacturers. It is one of the cases in which consideration has to be had to American legislation.

Again on January 10, 1907, the addition, at the close of subsection 6 of the anti-dumping clause, of the words "under like conditions having regard to the custom and usage of the trade," following the words "offered for sale to all purchasers on equal terms," was thus referred to by Mr. Fielding:[3]

It might be said that "equal terms" would mean that everybody must get the article at the same price. Of course, that is not the custom of trade.

---
[1] Debates in House of Commons, Dominion of Canada, session 1906-7, vol. 1, p. 1187.
[2] Debates in House of Commons, Dominion of Canada, session 1906-7, vol. 1, p. 1207-1208.
[3] Debates in House of Commons, Dominion of Canada, session 1906-7, vol. 1, p. 1230.

ADMINISTRATION OF THE PRESENT CANADIAN ANTI-DUMPING CLAUSE.

Explanatory of the operation of the present Canadian law, there will be found in the appendix of this report[1] sections of the customs act of Canada relating to the value for duty and the powers of the minister of customs, collectors and appraisers in determining values; the form of invoice required for goods sold by an exporter prior to shipment; and regulations issued by the Canadian department of customs. In brief, the administrative conditions and procedure are these:

The provisions of the anti-dumping law are enforced under the direction of the commissioner of customs in Canada, who issues regulations and other instructions to collectors of customs at the various ports of entry. The Canadian importer, who is the only party to foreign transactions within the jurisdiction of Canada, is made legally responsible for making customs entries. He is required to present an invoice, showing the actual price at which he purchased the goods he imports, and to swear that the value for duty stated in his entry is the fair market value of the goods, when sold for home consumption in the country of export. Two copies of each invoice must be presented. One is retained at the port of entry; the other is sent to the office of the department of customs at Ottawa.

The dumping duty, if any, is applied by the collectors of customs when the imported goods are entered. The invoice form certified by the foreign exporter is annexed to the entry when the papers are sworn to before the collector. The invoice furnished by the exporter to the Canadian importer contains two columns, one showing the fair market value of the merchandise, as sold for home consumption in the country of export; the other showing the selling price to the Canadian importer. If there is a difference in these prices beyond the exemption allowed (5 per cent, or as the case may be) under the regulations, the dumping duty is imposed by the collector.

The value for duty purposes in Canada is the value of the goods as sold for home consumption in the country of export. After the entry is made the papers go to the appraisers, who decide, on such information as they have, whether the values are correctly stated in the invoice. At important ports, such as Montreal, there are various appraisers who determine values. Each is a specialist in a particular class of goods. As aids in determining the value of the goods for home consumption in the country of export, the department of customs employs special customs officers, who are stationed in foreign countries. Four such special customs officers are located at important centers in the United States, and before the war there were two such officers in Europe; one in England, another on the Continent. In all cases referred to them the special customs officers visit the exporter and request permission to examine the exporter's books for the purpose of ascertaining the value of the goods for home consumption; or, in other words, the prices at which the goods are sold to home trade. These prices are compared with the prices at which the goods were sold to the Canadian importer. In the experience of the Canadian customs, very few exporters have refused this information. If an

---

[1] See Appendix pp. 35-38.

exporter declines to permit examination of his books, the dumping duty is applied, and if it is found on investigation after the goods are delivered that they are subject to dumping duties, the collector notifies the importer to pay the duties assessed.

In order to guard against evasion of the payment of the dumping duty by shipment of goods on consignment without sale prior to such shipment, it is provided that goods sold prior to shipment, but declared as consignments, are subject to such action as is deemed necessary to collect the special duty which would have been payable had the goods been sold to an importer prior to their shipment to Canada.

The appraisers of the Canadian customs department have accumulated considerable information in regard to the prices of many classes of commodities and are often able to determine at once the fair market value of merchandise; but hearings are usually granted to dissatisfied parties by the commissioner of customs, and a special agent is sometimes sent to make additional investigations if there appears to be reason for believing that the department has been misinformed as to the home market value of merchandise.

CANADIAN CLAUSE A CHECK ON DUMPING RATHER THAN A SOURCE OF REVENUE.

As evidence that the anti-dumping clause serves as a check on dumping rather than as a revenue producer, Canadian customs officials point to the following table, which shows that, in the 11 years from 1907 to 1918, inclusive, the Canadian dumping duties have averaged less than one-tenth of 1 per cent of the total duties collected.

Total duties and dumping duties—A comparison of latter to former collected on articles shipped to Canada, fiscal year ending Mar. 31.

Year.	Dumping duties collected.	Total duties collected.	Dumping duty per cent of total duty.	Year.	Dumping duties collected.	Total duties collected.	Dumping duty per cent of total duty.
1907	$94,649	[1] $40,290,172	0.23	1913	$88,963	$115,063,688	0.08
1908	52,688	58,331,075	.09	1914	92,426	107,180,578	.09
1909	47,722	48,059,792	.10	1915	68,290	[2] 79,205,910	.09
1910	54,796	61,024,239	.09	1916	69,143	[2] 103,940,101	.07
1911	53,912	73,312,368	.07	1917	91,715	[2] 147,631,455	.06
1912	86,354	87,576,037	.10	1918	58,478	[2] 161,595,629	.03

[1] Nine months ending Mar. 31, 1907.
[2] Includes war tax of the following amounts: 1915, $2,638,493; 1916, $25,256,788; 1917, $37,830,427; 1918, $45,018,562.

EFFECTIVENESS OF PRESENT CANADIAN ANTI-DUMPING LAW.

The following representative opinions on the effectiveness of the present Canadian anti-dumping law were expressed in Canada, in 1918, to the Tariff Commission's representative:

A prominent United States official in Canada.—It has never been attempted to make this provision of the tariff a revenue producer, but to have it operate as an additional protection in connection with the customs tariff. It is my impression and understanding that the Anti-Dumping Clause as applied by the Canadian Government has been, on the whole, satisfactory.

A leading Canadian customs official.—The Canadian Dumping Act has proved satisfactory as a general rule in securing the invoicing of goods for export to Canada at the same prices as they are sold to the home trade subject to the exemption allowance of 5 per cent, or as the case may be.

Former secretary, Canadian Manufacturers' Association.—The tendency has been that the exporter or shipper of goods charged more for his product when exported to Canada than before the dumping clause was put into effect. It has aided, by its deterrent effect, the building up of Canadian manufactures.

(This informant stated that the law would be much improved by the adoption of the following amendment:

The value for duty of articles imported should not in any case be less than the cost of production, plus a reasonable margin for profit).

Rubber goods manufacturer.—Since the war the dumping law has been enforced. Rubber goods, including rubber caps, etc., formerly imported, have been practically excluded by the dumping clause.

Hardware association president.—The working of the Anti-Dumping Law is satisfactory now. In the wholesale hardware business it tends to increase prices to Canada and to decrease trade with the United States. On the whole, Canadian goods are not so good as those brought from the United States.

Manager of a leading popular department store.—No Canadian merchant of importance doubts that the Dumping Law can be and is enforced. The Dumping Law has actually increased prices. In normal times the law would seriously affect the trade of Canada with the United States. We import from the United States women's wearing apparel, furniture, hosiery, jewelry, leather goods, and other goods. The Canadian customs officials knowing the American connections of this company, scrutinize its invoices very closely and increase the dumping duty whenever they can by increasing the value of the merchandise. The effect has been that the company has stopped looking for cheap merchandise from the United States and won't permit its buyers to get these bargains on account of the increased values added to the invoices by the customs people.

Shoe manufacturer.—Our traveling salesmen complain of (the importation of) cheap shoes from the United States and the Government seems to be unable to stop it.

Importer of steel plates, shapes, and tubes.—We formerly bought all our goods from the United States, now very little owing to the tariff and the Dumping Act. The Act is bad for the United States and Canada. If it were abolished trade would be greater with the United States. From an economic point of view, the dumping law is absolutely unsound. I would abolish it absolutely. It tends to monopoly and high protection even beyond the tariff. It is in restraint of trade. We are importers from the United States of steel plates, shapes, and tubes, for structural and other purposes. American goods are preferred by most buyers on account of their superior qualities.

Proprietor of high-grade department store.—When the manufacturer is protected by dumping clauses and embargoes, the losses occasioned by the inefficiency of the manufacturer are sustained by the consumer. By reason of the expertness, better equipment, organization, and general efficiency of American manufacturers as shown in women's garments, boots and shoes, and other goods, the Canadian demand for such merchandise is very strong, and the removal of the dumping clause, so far as these goods are concerned, would be the means not only of enabling Canadian women to satisfy their desires at less cost, but also of spurring manufacturers in Canada to greater efforts and bring them more quickly up to the same plane of efficiency.

VARIOUS ASPECTS OF ANTI-DUMPING LEGISLATION IN CANADA SOUTH AFRICA, AUSTRALIA, AND THE UNITED STATES.

It may be useful to consider briefly certain features of the Canadian law in connection with existing antidumping legislation of other countries, including the United States.[1]

So far, the experience of Canada supports the conclusion that the Canadian clause, in the main, has achieved its purpose. It may,

---

[1] Section IV, paragraph R, of the tariff act of 1913 (for text, see Appendix, p. 45), as it originally passed the House of Representatives, substantially repeated the Canadian anti-dumping clause. The section was stricken out by the Senate, which substituted a provision against unfair discrimination. This latter section was eliminated in conference.

however, remain doubtful whether the conditions under which the Canadian law has operated are comparable to those which now confront the United States, and, presumably, will be met in the near future by Canada. Enforcement is secured through customs officials of the Dominion, whose authority, in most instances, has enabled them, even extra-territorially, to procure dependable information on values. This facility in administration has been partly due to the circumstance that, until now, the major part of the shipments which the Canadian clause has been used to restrain, originated in the United States. Obtaining access to the exporters' books has been, therefore, a relatively simple process, enforceable, for the most part, by the intimation that the dumping duty would be assessed on the goods of exporters who declined to furnish the legally required information. If the United States enacts a similar statute, it may find a different and more complex task presented by the world-wide foreign prices of imported articles, especially those of Continental Europe and the Orient. It also remains to be seen whether effective methods of evasion of such statutes will not hereafter be devised.

Interesting questions are raised by the use in the Canadian clause of the expression "fair market value, applied to goods in the country of exportation," as the basis of the dumping duty. The phrase "actual market value" in the tariff laws of the United States (Section III, paragraphs K, L, and R, tariff act of 1913) has so well recognized a significance in customs administration in this country that customs officials are not favorable to the substitution of the Canadian language. Artificially lowered foreign market values, which might appear to be "actual" under the laws of the United States, might be deemed unfair by Canadian customs officials. Also, the simultaneous domestic and foreign dumping of the same products might pass muster under "actual" value tests, yet fail to succeed in the country of importation under the "fair" value test. Seemingly, too, the Canadian provision enables customs officials in determining foreign values to include drawbacks and foreign excises, except, under the law, in the case of excises on goods imported under the British preferential tariff.[1] Indeed, it would appear that by these very means the Canadian law has been used to create an added imperial preference and against importations from the United States. Moreover, while "actual market value" is only concerned with existing foreign conditions, the "fair market value" in cases of domestic necessity may reasonably sanction lower import prices than those prevailing abroad. On the other hand, by the application of its test to the time of exportation rather than sale the Canadian law appears poorly adapted to cases where the foreign market value is normally depressed, as, for instance, when seasonal articles, particularly toward the close of the season, are sharply declining in price.

The last preceding illustration directly raises another question. It is whether, notwithstanding the statutory limitations and the exercise of considerable administrative discretion, the Canadian law does not, at times, unduly increase to consumers the prices charged for certain imported commodities. The opinions of the operation and effects of the Canadian law given in this report are not devoid of complaints

---
[1] By Canada's Customs Memorandum, No. 2307 B, dated Apr. 15, 1919, it is for the time being provided that the dumping duty shall not apply in respect of foreign excise taxes.

from this standpoint, and should be carefully weighed. In certain respects the Canadian clause shows regard for the lowering of domestic prices; for example, by limiting its application, with a few specified exceptions, to all free and dutiable goods, "of a class or kind made or produced in Canada." The quoted qualification is favorable to benefits derived by consumers from any dumping of articles not thus made or produced. Yet it still may be questioned whether the public interest is wholly served by penalizing, to the extent approved in Canada, the importation at low prices of articles on the free list, domestically made or produced. Such problems as domestic conservation, foreign and domestic monopolies, and the welfare of consumers are involved. Some consequences of too sweeping an enactment are further avoided in Canada by the provision that the minister of customs by regulations may allow the temporary exemption of goods from the dumping duty if the minister is satisfied that similar articles are not made or sold in Canada in substantial quantities and that the imported goods are offered for sale to all purchasers on equal terms, under like conditions, having regard to the customs and usages of trade. In the absence of corresponding reservations the tendency of such legislation would be to deprive consumers, by precluding sale, of imported and even non-competitive articles at prices generally lower than the foreign levels. The field is one in which the public policy involved is somewhat varied by the nature of the commodities affected.

In considering similar legislation for the United States another flexible feature of the Canadian law is worthy of attention. It allows the temporary exemption of articles from the dumping duty when the difference between the fair market value abroad and the selling price to the importer is only a small percentage of the fair market value. Under this provision the Canadian regulations at present exempt goods from the dumping duty when such difference does not exceed 5 per cent of their fair market value. This per cent is subject to modification, and, because of constitutional limitations, care is required in drafting an equally elastic provision for the United States.

The other qualifications specified in the Canadian clause, which it is unnecessary to restate, should be similarly noted in conjunction with regulations modifying the application of the law.

The anti-dumping statute of the Union of South Africa [1] in essentials corresponds to that of Canada. In Australia, however, a different theory was adopted and a different practice inaugurated. Canada and South Africa strike at dumping directly as a separate evil. In contrast, the Industries Preservation Act of Australia [2] treats dumping as merely one phase of unfair competition.[3] Under the method there adopted, relief is afforded, after investigation, by a justice of the high court, who acts on the request of the controller general, after written complaint to the latter official that goods are being imported with intent unfairly to injure or destroy an Aus-

---

[1] Appendix, pp. 36-39.
[2] Appendix, pp. 39-42.
[3] New Zealand, in its monopoly prevention act of 1905 (New Zealand Consolidated Statutes, 1908, Vol. IV, pp. 283-285), provided for the payment of bonuses to manufacturers injured by the unfair competition of importers of agricultural implements, machines, and appliances. This portion of the act, which was essentially anti-dumping in character, though of limited duration, was subsequently continued in effect until December 31, 1915. Press reports (1919) quote the Minister for Customs as having said in a public address that the New Zealand Government has considered and drafted an anti-dumping clause for submission to Parliament when opportunity arises.

tralian industry. The findings of the justice are final and unappealable, and the imports deemed offensive may suffer the imposition of such conditions, including prohibition, as the justice may consider proper, subject to their modification by proclamation of the governor general. In principle, the Australian procedure is not dissimilar to that authorized for our Federal Trade Commission, which, in its supervision of unfair methods of competition, investigates, makes findings of fact, which are by law conclusive, if supported by evidence, and orders discontinuance of practices it adjudges unfair, subject to review by the Circuit Court of Appeals.[1]

The anti-dumping law enacted by Congress on September 8, 1916, invites special comment.[2] Some brief but substantial criticism of its effectiveness will be found among complaints presented to the commission and summarized in this report. As a criminal statute that act[3] must be strictly construed. It is wanting in certainty in providing, as a condition precedent of the conviction of offenders, that the sale of articles in the United States must be at a price "substantially less" than the actual market value or wholesale price abroad. It apparently fails, where the Canadian law succeeds, in not contemplating in reasonable cases the prohibition of sporadic dumping, since its penalties apply only to persons who "commonly and systematically import" foreign articles, and in providing that such importation must be made with intent to injure, destroy, or prevent the establishment of an industry in this country, or to monopolize trade or commerce in the imported articles. Evidently, for the most part, the language of the act makes difficult, if not impossible, the conviction of offenders and, for that reason, the enforcement of its purpose.

These defects in the statute somewhat support the contention that administrative remedies to prevent dumping are superior to criminal laws. If the act of 1916 is adhered to, attention should be devoted to the careful revision and strengthening of its provisions. Such amendment would not be inconsistent with the enactment of definite and authoritative instructions to the Federal Trade Commission to deal with dumping as a phase of unfair competitive methods. If preferred, some official body other than that commission might be vested with such jurisdiction. Furthermore, as separate or supplementary legislation, it is practicable by act of Congress to require some Federal body to investigate and report on specific complaints of dumping; also to instruct the President or Secretary of the Treasury to impose additional duties or refuse entry whenever the exist-

---

[1] For section 5 of the Federal Trade Commission act, see Appendix, pp. 42-3.
[2] There is some difference of opinion among the various trade committees as to the relative merits of the above-quoted legislative enactments of Canada and the United States, and the lines on which legislation having a similar object should proceed in the United Kingdom. The United States enactment is so recent (1916) and has come into force at such an exceptional time that there has been no experience of its working; but we are inclined to think that though the enactment has the advantage that it puts the responsibility of decision upon a judicial tribunal and not, as in Canada, upon an administrative authority, the requirement of proof that any "dumping" had, in fact, been done with intent to destroy or injure an industry in the United States, or prevent the development of an industry, may seriously limit its effect. * * * And, on the whole, we recommend that legislative action for the prevention of "dumping" be taken in the United Kingdom on the lines (though not necessarily in the precise form) adopted in Canada, but we see no reason why the "anti-dumping" duty should be restricted, as in that Dominion, to 15 per cent. We think it should be equivalent to the full difference between the "selling price" and the "fair market value," however large that difference may be. * * * Final Report of the Committee On Commercial and Industrial Policy After The War, par. 221-222 (London, 1918).
[3] Appendix, p. 42.

ence of dumping in any industrially destructive form is established. In lieu of the refusal of entry, bonds to secure the payment of possible dumping duties may be required from importers. Such legislation, which would conform to American precedents and established customs practices, would make possible flexibility of administration, the prevention alike of sporadic and persistent dumping, and some safeguarding of consumers against conceivable efforts artificially and unnecessarily to raise prices.

The act of September 8, 1916, expresses the repressive purpose of Congress, and the commission concludes that the somewhat meager evidence at hand of the extent to which dumping is being practiced in this country does not lessen the wisdom of further legislation. The usage is well established, its train of consequences obvious, and the prevention of its abuses sensible. Another statute may reasonably impose added restrictions.

APPENDIX.

Valuation for Duty, and Powers of Appraisers, Collectors and the Minister of Customs in Determining Values Under the Customs Act of Canada.[1]

VALUATION FOR DUTY.

SEC. 40. Whenever any duty *ad valorem* is imposed on any goods imported into Canada, the value for duty shall be the fair market value thereof, when sold for home consumption, in the principal markets of the country whence and at the time when the same were exported directly to Canada. * * *.

SEC. 41. Such market value shall be the fair market value of such goods, in the usual and ordinary commercial acceptation of the term and as sold in the ordinary course of trade: Provided that a discount for cash, for duty purposes, shall not exceed two and one-half per cent and shall not be allowed unless it has been actually allowed and deducted by the exporter on the invoice to the importer. * * *.

SEC. 43. The Dominion Customs appraisers and every one of them and every person who acts as such appraiser, or the collector of Customs, as the case may be, shall, by all reasonable ways and means in his or their power, ascertain, estimate and appraise the true and fair market value (any invoice or affidavit thereto to the contrary notwithstanding), of the goods at the time of exportation and in the principal markets of the country whence the same have been imported into Canada, and the proper weights, measures or other quantities, and the fair market value thereof, as the case requires.

2. In the case of goods shipped to Canada on consignment, but sold by the exporter to persons in Canada prior to their importation into Canada, the amount of the valuation for duty shall not be less than the invoice value to the Canadian purchaser, exclusive of all charges upon the goods, after shipment from the place whence exported directly into Canada.

3. When articles of the same material, or of a similar kind but of a different quality, are found in the same package, charged or invoiced at an average price, the appraisers shall adopt the value of the best article contained in such package as the average value of the whole; and duty shall be levied thereon accordingly. * * *.

VALUE FOR DUTY UNDER SPECIAL CONDITIONS.

SEC. 44. The fair market value of goods shall be taken to include the amount of any drawback which has been allowed by the Government of any other country, also the amount of consideration or money value of any special arrangement between the exporter and the importer or between any persons interested therein because of the exportation or intended exportation of such goods, or the right to territorial limits for the sale or use thereof, and also the amount or money value of any so-called royalty, rent or charge for use of any machine or goods of any description, which the seller or proprietor does or would usually charge thereon when the same are sold or leased or rented for use in the country whence they have been exported to Canada.

2. When the amount of such drawback, consideration, money value, royalty, rent or charge for use has been deducted from the value of such goods, on the face of the invoice under which entry is to be made, or is not shown thereon, the collector of Customs or proper officer shall add the amount of such deduction, drawback, consideration, money value, royalty, rent or charge for use, and cause to be paid the lawful duty thereon. * * *

SEC. 45. No deduction of any kind shall be allowed from the value of any goods imported into Canada, because of any drawback paid or to be paid thereon, or because of any special arrangement between the seller and purchaser having reference to the exportation of such goods, or the exclusive right to territorial limits for the sale thereof, or because of any royalty payable upon patent rights, but not payable when the goods are purchased for exportation, or on account of any other consideration

---

[1] Revised Statutes of Canada, 1906, as amended, published by the Department of Customs, 1914, pp. 14-16.

by which a special reduction in price might or could be obtained: Provided that nothing in this section shall be understood to apply to general fluctuations of market values. * * *

SEC. 46. Whenever goods are imported into Canada under such circumstances or conditions as render it difficult to determine the value thereof for duty because—

(a) Such goods are not sold for use or consumption in the country of production; or,

(b) A lease of such goods or the right of using the same but not the right of property therein is sold or given; or,

(c) Such goods having a royalty imposed thereon, the royalty is uncertain, or is not from other causes a reliable means of estimating the value of the goods; or,

(d) Such goods are usually or exclusively sold by or to agents or by subscription; or,

(e) Such goods are sold or imported in or under any other unusual or peculiar manner or conditions;

the minister may determine the value for duty of such goods, and the value so determined shall, until otherwise provided, be the value upon which the duty on such goods shall be computed and levied.

2. The minister shall be the sole judge as to the existence of all or any of the causes or reasons aforesaid. * * *

DUTIABLE CHARGES.

SEC. 48. No deduction from the value of goods contained in any invoice shall be allowed on account of the assumed value of any package or packages, where no charge for such package or packages has been made in such invoice; and where such charge is made the Customs officer shall see that the charge is fair and reasonable, and represents no more than the original cost thereof. * * *

SEC. 49. No deduction from the value of goods in any invoice shall be made on account of charges for packing, or for straw, twine, cord, paper, cording, wiring or cutting, or for any expense incurred or said to have been incurred in the preparation and packing of goods for shipment, and all such charges and expenses shall, in all cases, be included as part of the value for duty. * * *

Canadian Customs Regulations Issued in 1914.[1]

DEPARTMENT OF CUSTOMS, CANADA.

Ottawa, 24th August, 1914.

To Collectors of Customs and others concerned:

NEW REGULATIONS UNDER THE CUSTOMS DUMPING CLAUSE.

The regulations heretofore made as to exemptions from customs special duty (or dumping duty) under paragraph (7) of section 6 of the Customs Tariff, 1907, as set forth in Memo. 1407 B, Memo. 1506 B, and Memo. No. 1652 B, are repealed and the following regulations are made and established in place thereof—in effect 1st September, 1914, viz:

Under the special duty provisions of the customs tariff, the special duty (or dumping duty) is not to apply in the following cases, viz:

(a) When the difference between the fair market value and the selling price of the goods to the importer in Canada does not exceed 5 per cent of their fair market value.

Provided that the whole difference shall be taken into account for special duty purposes when exceeding 5 per cent.

Provided, further, that special duty or dumping duty under the Customs Tariff shall without exemption allowance apply to articles of a class or kind made in Canada when admitted free of ordinary duty and shall also apply without exemption allowance to round rolled wire rods of iron or steel.

JOHN MCDOUGALD,
Commissioner of Customs.

REGULATIONS BY ORDER IN COUNCIL AND BY THE DEPARTMENT OF CUSTOMS RESPECTING INVOICES, ENTRIES, AND SPECIAL DUTY OR DUMPING DUTY.

1. Invoices in duplicate properly certified shall be delivered at the custom house with the bills of entry for all imported goods.

2. Every such invoice shall contain a sufficient and correct description of the goods, and in respect of goods sold by the exporter shall show in one column the actual price

---

[1] Customs Memorandum No. 1812 B, Department of Customs, Ottawa, Canada, Aug. 24, 1914.

at which the articles have been sold to the importer, and in a separate column the fair market value of each article as sold for home consumption in the country of export.

3. The "*price*" and "*value*" of goods in every case aforesaid are to be stated as in condition packed ready for shipment at the time when, and at the place whence, the goods have been exported directly to Canada.

4. When the value of goods for duty purposes is determined by the Minister of Customs under the provisions of the customs act, by reason of the goods being exported or imported under unusual conditions, the value so determined shall be held to be the fair market value thereof.

5. In making customs entry the "Special duty" may be shown by itself in the "net duty" column of the entry on the line below the article subject to special duty or on the line below continuous numbers of articles subject to special duty.

6. Goods of a class or kind made in Canada are subject to special duty, when sold for exportation to Canada at a less price than for home consumption in the country of export, whether such goods be otherwise free of duty or subject to specific or *ad valorem duties*—with the exceptions stated in clause 6 of the tariff as hereinbefore quoted.

7. *By regulations in force from 1st September, 1914.*—Under the special duty provisions of the customs tariff, the special duty (or dumping duty) is not to apply in the following cases, viz:

(a) When the difference between the fair market value and the selling price of the goods to the importer in Canada does not exceed 5 per cent of their fair market value. Provided, that the whole difference shall be taken into account for special duty purposes when exceeding 5 per cent. Provided, further, that special duty or dumping duty under the customs tariff shall *without exemption allowance* apply to articles of a class or kind made in Canada when admitted free of ordinary duty and shall also without exemption allowance apply to round rolled wire rods of iron or steel.

8. *Bona fide samples admitted without special duty.*—Articles of merchandise for use *bona fide* as samples for sale of similar goods are to be admitted without *special duty*;— (subject, however, to *ordinary* duties as heretofore).

9. *Advance in market value after purchase of goods by importer not subject to special duty.*—The amount to any advance in the market value of goods between the time of their purchase by the importer and the date of their exportation to Canada shall not be subject to special duty after 9th November, 1904, provided the goods have been exported in the usual course and the actual date of purchase established to the satisfaction of the collector by contracts or other sufficient documents produced for his inspection and attested to.

Provided, however, in respect of goods subject to an *ad valorem* duty, that the *ordinary duty* shall be collected (as heretofore) on the fair market value of the goods as at the time of their direct exportation to Canada—under the provisions of Sections 40 and 41 of the Customs Act. (Revised Statutes of Canada, 1906, chapter 48.)

10. *Rule to be observed (for special duty purposes only) in comparing "fair market value" with export price.*—In computing the difference for special duty purposes between the "Fair Market Value" in the country of export and the "Selling price to the importer in Canada", the fair market value of goods is to be estimated on the usual credit basis, except when the article is universally sold in the country of export for cash only, in which case the fair market value is to be estimated on a cash basis;

Provided that a *bona fide* discount for cash not exceeding 2½ per cent when allowed and deducted by the exporter on his invoice may be allowed in estimating the fair market value of goods for duty purposes.

Examples:

(1) Hats sold for Home Consumption at $100 on credit, subject to 7 per cent *Cash* discount, would be liable to Special duty if sold to a purchaser in Canada on usual credit at $93, but would not be liable to special duty if sold to a purchaser in Canada for $93 cash.

(2) Machinery sold for Home Consumption at $100 on Credit, subject to 2½ per cent *Cash* discount, would not be liable to Special duty if sold to a purchaser in Canada for $93 Cash, as the "difference" does not exceed 5 per cent after raising the *Cash* price ($93) by 2½ per cent to its *Credit* equivalent.

JOHN MCDOUGALD,
Commissioner of Customs.

Specimen Form of Canadian invoice, Approved by the Canadian Department of Customs for Goods Sold by Exporter Prior to Shipment.

(Place and date) ....

Invoice of .... purchased

by   of
....

from   of
....

to be shipped from   per
....

Marks and numbers on packages.	Quantities and description of goods.	Fair market value as sold for home consumption at time shipped.	Selling price to the purchaser in Canada.	
			@	Amount.

(Signature of seller or agent) ....

Anti-dumping Legislation of the Union of South Africa.[1]

SEC. 7. For the purpose of estimating the amount of customs duty whenever levied on goods *ad valorem* and for the purpose of the declarations and oaths which may at any time be required by law or regulation in relation to the question of such duty, the value for purposes of duty of those goods shall be taken to be the true current value for home consumption in the open market of similar goods in the principal markets of the country from which, and at the time at which, the goods were imported, including carriage to the port of shipment and the cost of packing and packages, but not including agents' commission when such commission does not exceed 5 per cent: *Provided*, That in no case shall the value for purposes of duty, as in this section defined, be less than the cost of the goods to the importer at the port of shipment.

SEC. 8. Anything to the contrary notwithstanding in this act contained, the following provisions shall be in force in respect of the charging, levying, collection, and payment of customs duty:

(1) In the case of goods imported into the Union of a class or kind made or produced in the Union, if the export or actual selling price to an importer in the Union be less than the true current value (as defined in this act) of the same goods when sold for home consumption in the usual and ordinary course in the country from which they were exported to the Union at the time of their exportation thereto, there may, in addition to the duties otherwise prescribed, be charged, levied, collected, and paid on those goods on importation into the Union a special customs duty (or dumping duty) equal to the difference between the said selling price of the goods for export and the true current value thereof for home consumption as defined in this act: *Provided*, That the special customs duty (or dumping duty) shall not in any case exceed 15 per cent *ad valorem*.

[1] From The International Customs Journal, also entitled "Bulletin International Des Douanes" No. 42, published by the International Customs Tariffs Bureau, year 1914-15 No. 42, entitled "The Union of South Africa," 6th ed., Brussels, August, 1914. The title of the act of the Union of South Africa is given as follows: "Act to provide for the imposition of duties of customs upon goods imported into the Union and for the licensing of customs merchants, and to empower the governor general to enter into agreements relating to customs with the governments of every Territory, State, or Protectorate in South Africa." (No. 26, 1914, assented to July 7, 1914.)

(2) When a bounty is granted in the country of origin on any goods of a class or kind made or produced in the Union an additional customs duty equal to the amount of such bounty may be charged, levied, and collected upon the importation of those goods into the Union.

(3) The goods in respect of which there may be charged, levied, and collected any special (or dumping) customs duty under subsection (1) or any additional customs duty under subsection (2) shall be from time to time determined by the governor general and notified by him by proclamation in the Gazette, together with the date as from which such his determination shall take effect: *Provided*, That such date shall not be less than six weeks after the publication of the proclamation.

Anti-dumping Legislation of Australia.[1]

The act is entitled "An act for the preservation of Australian industries and for the repression of destructive monopolies." It was assented to September 24, 1906, and subsequently amended in 1908, 1909, and 1910. It is divided into three parts as follows: I, Preliminary; II, Repression of monopolies; III, Prevention of dumping. It defines a "commercial trust" as including a combination whose voting powers of determination are controlled or controllable (among other things) by an agreement or similar means. Part II, among other things, declares any person whose principal or agent engages in a combination, or enters into a contract to restrain trade, or by means of unfair competition to destroy or injure any Australian industry advantageous to the Commonwealth having due regard for the interests of producers, workers, and consumers, is guilty of an offense with a penalty of £500, and if continuing, with such penalty for each day of the offense.

By an amendment of 1910, it was provided that it should be a defense to a charge of restraint or attempted restraint of trade if the defendant proves that the thing complained of was not a detriment to the public, and that the restraint was not unreasonable.

By section 6 of the act, unfair competition is defined as follows:

"(1) For the purposes of section 4 and section 10 of this Act, unfair competition means competition which is unfair in the circumstances; and in the following cases the competition shall be deemed to be unfair unless the contrary is proved:—

"(a) If the defendant is a Commercial Trust:

"(b) If the competition would probably or does in fact result in an inadequate remuneration for labor in the Australian industry:

"(c) If the competition would probably or does in fact result in creating substantial disorganization in Australian industry or throwing workers out of employment:

"(d) If the defendant, with respect to any goods or services which are the subject of the competition, gives, offers, or promises to any person any rebate, refund, discount, or reward upon condition that that person deals, or in consideration of that person having dealt, with the defendant to the exclusion of other persons dealing in similar goods or services.

"(2) In determining whether the competition is unfair, regard shall be had to the management, the processes, the plant, and the machinery employed or adopted in the Australian industry affected by the competition being reasonably efficient, effective, and up-to-date."

By section 7 of the act, monopoly, or attempted monopoly, of interstate or external trade is declared an indictable offense punishable both by a fine and imprisonment. By section 7a, the giving of rebates and concessions in interstate trade and with foreign countries is declared an offense punishable by fine.

It is provided both with respect to monopolies in restraint of trade within and without Australia, and to unfair concessions, that every contract in violation of the act shall be absolutely illegal and void. Section 7b makes it an offense punishable by fine to refuse absolutely or only on disadvantageous conditions to sell to other persons. Section 9 makes those who aid and abet in the offenses mentioned likewise guilty of an offense punishable by fine. Contracts may be enjoined in the high court, in proceedings instituted by the attorney general or any person authorized by him, in the case of commerce between States or with other countries. Disobedience of an injunction is punishable. It is further provided that any person injured by any act in

---

[1] The Australian Industries Preservation Act, 1906-10, Commonwealth Acts (Australia), 1901-11, Vol II, pp. 1018-1030.

contravention may sue for and recover treble damages. This portion of the act also gives power to the comptroller general to require persons to answer questions and produce documents.

Part III of the act, which appears to have remained without amendment, as passed in 1906 is as follows:

"PART III.—PREVENTION OF DUMPING.

"16. In this Part of this Act 'justice' means a Justice of the high court; 'the Comptroller-General' means the Comptroller-General of Customs; 'Imported goods' and 'Australian goods' include goods of those classes respectively, and all parts or ingredients thereof; 'Produced' includes manufactured, and 'Producer' includes manufacturer; 'Trade' includes production of every kind; 'Industries' shall not include industries in which, in the opinion of the Comptroller-General or Justice as the case may be, the majority of workers do not receive adequate remuneration or are subject to unfair terms or conditions of labor or employment.

"17. Unfair competition has in all cases reference to competition with those Australian industries, the preservation of which, in the opinion of the Comptroller-General or a Justice as the case may be, is advantageous to the Commonwealth, having due regard to the interests of producers, workers, and consumers.

"18. (1) For the purposes of this Part of this Act, competition shall be deemed to be unfair, unless the contrary is proved, if (a) under ordinary circumstances of trade it would probably lead to the Australian goods being no longer produced or being withdrawn from the market or being sold at a loss unless produced at an inadequate remuneration for labor; or (b) the means adopted by the person importing or selling the imported goods are, in the opinion of the Comptroller-General or a Justice, as the case may be, unfair in the circumstances; or (c) the competition would probably or does in fact result in an inadequate remuneration for labor in the Australian industry; or (d) the competition would probably or does in fact result in creating any substantial disorganization in Australian industry or throwing workers out of employment; or (e) the imported goods have been purchased abroad by or for the importer, from the manufacturer or some person acting for or in combination with him or accounting to him, at prices greatly below their ordinary cost of production where produced or market price where purchased; or (f) the imported goods are imported by or for the manufacturer, or some person acting for or in combination with him or accounting to him, and are being sold in Australia at a price which is less than gives the person importing or selling them a fair profit upon their fair foreign market value, or their fair selling value if sold in the country of production, together with all charges after shipment from the place whence the goods are exported directly to Australia (including customs duty).

"(2) In determining whether the competition is unfair, regard shall be had to the management, the processes, the plant, and the machinery employed or adopted in the Australian industry affected by the competition being reasonably efficient, effective, and up-to-date.

"19. (1) The Comptroller-General, whenever he has received a complaint in writing and has reason to believe that any person (hereinafter called the importer), either singly or in combination with any other person within or beyond the Commonwealth, is importing into Australia goods (hereinafter called imported goods) with intent to destroy or injure any Australian industry by their sale or disposal within the Commonwealth in unfair competition with any Australian goods, may certify to the Minister accordingly.

"(2) The certificate of the Comptroller-General shall specify (a) the imported goods; (b) the Australian industry and goods; (c) the importer; (d) the grounds of unfairness in the competition; (e) the name, address, and occupation of any person (not being an officer of the public service) upon whose information he may have acted.

"(3) The Comptroller-General may add to his certificate a statement of such other facts as in his opinion ought to be specified to give the importer fair notice of the matters complained of.

"(4) The Comptroller-General shall, before making his certificate, give to the importer an opportunity to show cause why the certificate should not be made and furnish him with a copy of the complaint.

"(5) On receipt of the certificate the Minister may (a) by order in writing refer to a Justice the investigation and determination of the question whether the imported goods are being imported with the intent alleged; and, if so, whether the importation of the goods should be prohibited either absolutely or subject to any specified conditions or restrictions or limitations; (b) notify in the *Gazette* that the question has been so referred; and (c) forward to the Justice a copy of the certificate.

DUMPING AND UNFAIR FOREIGN COMPETITION. 41

"20. From the date of the *Gazette* notice until the publication in the *Gazette* of the determination of the question by the Justice, goods the subject of the investigation shall not be imported unless the importer (a) gives to the Minister a bond with such sureties as the Minister approves, for such amount (not exceeding the true value of the goods for customs purposes) as the Minister considers just and reasonable by way of precaution in the circumstances, and conditioned to be void if the Justice determines the question in favor of the importer; or (b) gives such other security and complies with such other conditions as the Minister approves; and those goods shall, if imported in contravention of this section, be deemed to be prohibited imports within the meaning of the *Customs Act* 1901, and the provisions of that Act shall apply to the goods accordingly.

"21. (1) The Justice shall proceed to expeditiously and carefully investigate and determine the matter, and for the purpose of the proceeding shall have power to inquire as to any goods, things, and matters whatsoever which he considers pertinent, necessary, or material.

"(2) For the purpose of the proceeding the Justice shall sit in open Court, and shall have all the powers of a Justice in the exercise of the ordinary jurisdiction of the High Court. He may, if he thinks fit, and shall on the application of either party, state a case for the opinion of the Full Court upon any question of law arising in the proceeding. And he may if he thinks fit, at any stage of the proceeding, refer the investigation and determination of the matter to the Full Court, which shall in that case have all the powers and functions of a Justice under this part of this act.

"(3) The certificate of the Comptroller-General shall be *prima facie* evidence of facts by subsection (2) of section 19 of this Act required to be specified therein.

"(4) In addition to the Comptroller-General and the importer the Justice may, if he thinks fit, allow any person interested in importing imported goods to be represented at the investigation.

"(5) The Justice shall be guided by good conscience and the substantial merits of the case, without regard to legal forms or technicalities, or whether the evidence before him is in accordance with the law of evidence or not.

"(6) No person shall in any proceeding before a Justice be excused from answering any question or producing documents on the ground that the answer or production may criminate or tend to criminate him, but his answer shall not be admissible in evidence against him in any criminal proceeding other than a prosecution for perjury.

"(7) The justice shall forward his determination to the Minister.

"(8) In the case of the following agricultural implements: Plows of all kinds over 1½ hundredweight, tine harrows, disk harrows, grain drills, combined grain seed and manure drills, land rollers, cultivators, chaff cutters, seed cleaners, stripper harvesters, and any other implement usually used in agriculture, the Justice shall inquire into and determine the question whether the goods are being imported with the effect of benefiting the primary producers without unfairly injuring any other section of the community of the Commonwealth.

"(9) The determination of the Justice shall be final and conclusive and without appeal, and shall not be questioned in any way.

"22. (1) Upon the receipt of the determination of the Justice, the Minister shall forthwith cause it to be published in the *Gazette*.

"(2) If the Justice determines that the imported goods are being imported with the intent alleged, and that their importation should be prohibited either absolutely or subject to any specified conditions or restrictions or limitations of any kind whatsoever: (a) The determination when so published shall have the effect of a proclamation under the *Customs Act* 1901 prohibiting the importation of the goods either absolutely or subject to those conditions or limitations as the case may be; and in that case the provisions of that Act shall apply to goods so prohibited; and (b) the Justice may by order reduce the amount recoverable under any bond given in pursuance of this Part of this Act to such sum as the importer satisfies him is reasonable and just in the circumstances.

"23. The Governor-General may at any time, by proclamation, simultaneously with or subsequently to any prohibition under this part of this Act, rescind in whole or in part, the prohibition or any condition or restriction or limitation on importation imposed thereby.

"24. In all cases of prohibition the determination of the Justice and any proclamation affecting the same shall be laid before both Houses of the Parliament within seven days after the publication in the *Gazette*, or. if the Parliament is not then sitting, within seven days after the next meeting of Parliament.

"25. The Justices of the High Court, or a majority of them, may make rules of Court, not inconsistent with this Act, for regulating the proceedings before a Justice under this Part of this Act. and for carrying this Part of this Act into effect.

"26. (1) Any person who willfully (a) makes to the Comptroller-General or to any officer of Customs any false statement in relation to any action or proceedings taken or proposed to be taken under this Part of this Act; or (b) misleads the Comptroller-General in any particular likely to affect the discharge of his duty under this Act, shall be guilty of an offense. Penalty: One hundred pounds or 12 months' imprisonment.

"(2) Any person convicted under the last preceding subsection may be ordered by the Justice to whom a question is referred under this Part of this Act to pay the whole or part of the costs incurred by the importer in whose favor the question is determined.

Antidumping Statute of the United States.[1]

SEC. 800. That when used in this title the term "person" includes partnerships, corporations, and associations.

SEC. 801. That it shall be unlawful for any person importing or assisting in importing any articles from any foreign country into the United States, commonly and systematically to import, sell, or cause to be imported or sold, such articles within the United States at a price substantially less than the actual market value or wholesale price of such articles, at the time of exportation to the United States, in the principal markets of the country of their production, or of other foreign countries to which they are commonly exported after adding to such market value or wholesale price, freight, duty, and other charges and expenses necessarily incident to the importation and sale thereof in the United States: *Provided*, That such act or acts be done with the intent of destroying or injuring an industry in the United States, or of preventing the establishment of an industry in the United States, or of restraining or monopolizing any part of trade and commerce in such articles in the United States.

Any person who violates or combines or conspires with any other person to violate this section is guilty of a misdemeanor, and, on conviction thereof, shall be punished by a fine not exceeding $5,000, or imprisonment not exceeding one year, or both, in the discretion of the court.

Any person injured in his business or property by reason of any violation of, or combination or conspiracy to violate this section, may sue therefor in the district court of the United States for the district in which the defendant resides or is found or has an agent, without respect to the amount in controversy, and shall recover threefold the damages sustained and the cost of the suit, including a reasonable attorney's fee.

The foregoing provisions shall not be construed to deprive the proper State courts of jurisdiction in actions for damages thereunder.

Section 5 of the Act Creating the Federal Trade Commission.[2]

SEC. 5. That unfair methods of competition in commerce are hereby declared unlawful.

The commission is hereby empowered and directed to prevent persons, partnerships, or corporations, except banks and common carriers subject to the Acts to regulate commerce, from using unfair methods of competition in commerce.

Whenever the commission shall have reason to believe that any such person, partnership, or corporation has been or is using any unfair method of competition in commerce, and if it shall appear to the commission that a proceeding by it in respect thereof would be to the interest of the public, it shall issue and serve upon such person, partnership, or corporation a complaint, stating its charges in that respect, and containing a notice of a hearing upon a day and at a place therein fixed at least thirty days after the service of said complaint. The person, partnership, or corporation so complained of shall have the right to appear at the place and time so fixed and show cause why an order should not be entered by the commission requiring such person, partnership, or corporation to cease and desist from the violation of the law so charged in said complaint. Any person, partnership, or corporation may make application, and upon good cause shown may be allowed by the commission, to intervene and appear in said proceeding by counsel or in person. The testimony in any such proceeding shall be reduced to writing and filed in the office of the commission. If upon such hearing the commission shall be of the opinion that the method

---

[1] Revenue act (64th Cong.), Sept. 8, 1916.
[2] Sixty-third Congress, approved Sept. 26, 1914.

of competition in question is prohibited by this Act, it shall make a report in writing in which it shall state its findings as to the facts, and shall issue and cause to be served on such person, partnership, or corporation an order requiring such person, partnership, or corporation to cease and desist from using such method of competition. Until a transcript of the record in such hearing shall have been filed in a circuit court of appeals of the United States, as hereinafter provided, the commission may at any time, upon such notice and in such manner as it shall deem proper, modify or set aside, in whole or in part, any report or any order made or issued by it under this section.

If such person, partnership, or corporation fails or neglects to obey such order of the commission while the same is in effect, the commission may apply to the circuit court of appeals of the United States, within any circuit where the method of competition in question was used or where such person, partnership, or corporation resides or carries on business, for the enforcement of its order, and shall certify and file with its application a transcript of the entire record in the proceeding, including all the testimony taken and the report and order of the commission. Upon such filing of the application and transcript the court shall cause notice thereof to be served upon such person, partnership, or corporation, and thereupon shall have jurisdiction of the proceeding and of the question determined therein, and shall have power to make and enter upon the pleadings, testimony, and proceedings set forth in such transcript a decree affirming, modifying, or setting aside the order of the commission. The findings of the commission as to the facts, if supported by testimony, shall be conclusive. If either party shall apply to the court for leave to adduce additional evidence, and shall show to the satisfaction of the court that such additional evidence is material and that there were reasonable grounds for the failure to adduce such evidence in the proceeding before the commission, the court may order such additional evidence to be taken before the commission and to be adduced upon the hearing in such manner and upon such terms and conditions as to the court may seem proper. The commission may modify its findings as to the facts, or make new findings, by reason of the additional evidence so taken, and it shall file such modified or new findings, which, if supported by testimony, shall be conclusive, and its recommendation, if any, for the modification or setting aside of its original order, with the return of such additional evidence. The judgment and decree of the court shall be final, except that the same shall be subject to review by the Supreme Court upon certiorari as provided in section two hundred and forty of the Judicial Code.

Any party required by such order of the commission to cease and desist from using such method of competition may obtain a review of such order in said circuit court of appeals by filing in the court a written petition praying that the order of the commission be set aside. A copy of such petition shall be forthwith served upon the commission, and thereupon the commission forthwith shall certify and file in the court a transcript of the record as hereinbefore provided. Upon the filing of the transcript the court shall have the same jurisdiction to affirm, set aside, or modify the order of the commission as in the case of an application by the commission for the enforcement of its order, and the findings of the commission as to the facts, if supported by testimony, shall in like manner be conclusive.

The jurisdiction of the circuit court of appeals of the United States to enforce, set aside, or modify orders of the commission shall be exclusive.

Such proceedings in the circuit court of appeals shall be given precedence over other cases pending therein, and shall be in every way expedited. No order of the commission or judgment of the court to enforce the same shall in any wise relieve or absolve any person, partnership, or corporation from any liability under the antitrust acts.

Complaints, orders, and other processes of the commission under this section may be served by anyone duly authorized by the commission, either (a) by delivering a copy thereof to the person to be served, or to a member of the partnership to be served, or to the president, secretary, or other executive officer or a director of the corporation to be served; or (b) by leaving a copy thereof at the principal office or place of business of such person, partnership, or corporation; or (c) by registering and mailing a copy thereof addressed to such person, partnership, or corporation at his or its principal office or place of business. The verified return by the person so serving said complaint, order, or other process setting forth the manner of said service shall be proof of the same, and the return post-office receipt for said complaint, order, or other process registered and mailed as aforesaid shall be proof of the service of the same.

44   UNITED STATES TARIFF COMMISSION REPORT.

Full Line Forcing Statute of the United States.[1]

SEC. 800. That when used in this title the term "person" includes partnerships, corporations, and associations.

* * * * * * *

SEC. 802. That if any article produced in a foreign country is imported into the United States under any agreement, understanding, or condition that the importer thereof or any other person in the United States shall not use, purchase, or deal in, or shall be restricted in his using, purchasing, or dealing in, the articles of any other person, there shall be levied, collected, and paid thereon, in addition to the duty otherwise imposed by law, a special duty equal to double the amount of such duty: *Provided*, That the above shall not be interpreted to prevent the establishing in this country on the part of a foreign producer of an exclusive agency for the sale in the United States of the products of said foreign producer or merchant, nor to prevent such exclusive agent from agreeing not to use, purchase, or deal in the article of any other person, but this proviso shall not be construed to exempt from the provisions of this section any article imported by such exclusive agent if such agent is required by the foreign producer or if it is agreed between such agent and such foreign producer that any agreement, understanding or condition set out in this section shall be imposed by such agent upon the sale or other disposition of such article to any person in the United States.

Provision for Countervailing Duties in the United States.[2]

"E. That whenever any country, dependency, colony, province, or other political subdivision of government shall pay or bestow, directly or indirectly, any bounty or grant upon the exportation of any article or merchandise from such country, dependency, colony, province, or other political subdivision of government, and such article or merchandise is dutiable under the provisions of this Act, then upon the importation of any such article or merchandise into the United States, whether the same shall be imported directly from the country of production or otherwise, and whether such article or merchandise is imported in the same condition as when exported from the country of production or has been changed in condition by remanufacture or otherwise, there shall be levied and paid, in all such cases, in addition to the duties otherwise imposed by this Act, an additional duty equal to the net amount of such bounty or grant, however the same be paid or bestowed. The net amount of all such bounties or grants shall be from time to time ascertained, determined, and declared by the Secretary of the Treasury, who shall make all needful regulations for the identification of such articles and merchandise and for the assessment and collection of such additional duties."

Undrvaluation Section of the Tariff Act of October 3, 1913.[3]

I. That the owner, consignee, or agent of any imported merchandise may, at the time when he shall make entry of such merchandise, but not after either the invoice or the merchandise has come under the observation of the appraiser, make such addition in the entry to or such deduction from the cost or value given in the invoice or pro forma invoice or statement in form of an invoice, which he shall produce with his entry, as in his opinion may raise or lower the same to the actual market value or wholesale price of such merchandise at the time of exportation to the United States, in the principal markets of the country from which the same has been imported; and the collector within whose district any merchandise may be imported or entered, whether the same has been actually purchased or procured otherwise than by purchase, shall cause the actual market value or wholesale price of such merchandise to be appraised; and if the appraised value of any article of imported merchandise subject to an ad valorem duty or to a duty based upon or regulated in any manner by the value thereof shall exceed the value declared in the entry, there shall be levied, collected, and paid, in addition to the duties imposed by law on such merchandise, an additional duty of 1 per centum of the total appraised value thereof for each 1 per centum that such appraised value exceeds the value declared in the entry: *Provided*, That the additional duties shall only apply to the particular article or articles in each invoice that are so undervalued and

---

[1] Revenue act (64th Cong.), Sept. 8, 1916.
[2] Paragraph E, Section IV, Tariff Act of Oct. 3, 1913.
[3] Section III, paragraph I, Tariff Act of October 3, 1913.

shall not be imposed upon any article upon which the amount of duty imposed by law on account of the appraised value does not exceed the amount of duty that would be imposed if the appraised value did not exceed the entered value, and shall be limited to 75 per centum of the appraised value of such article or articles. Such additional duties shall not be construed to be penal, and shall not be remitted nor payment thereof in any way avoided except in cases arising from a manifest clerical error, nor shall they be refunded in case of exportation of the merchandise, or on any other account, nor shall they be subject to the benefit of drawback: *Provided*, That if the appraised value of any merchandise shall exceed the value declared in the entry by more than 75 per centum, except when arising from a manifest clerical error, such entry shall be held to be presumptively fraudulent, and the collector of customs shall seize such merchandise and proceed as in case of forfeiture for violation of the customs laws, and in any legal proceeding other than a criminal prosecution that may result from such seizure, the undervaluation as shown by the appraisal shall be presumptive evidence of fraud, and the burden of proof shall be on the claimant to rebut the same, and forfeiture shall be adjudged unless he shall rebut such presumption of fraudulent intent by sufficient evidence. The forfeiture provided for in this section shall apply to the whole of the merchandise or the value thereof in the case or package containing the particular article or articles in each invoice which are undervalued: *Provided further*, That all additional duties, penalties, or forfeitures applicable to merchandise entered by a duly certified invoice shall be alike applicable to merchandise entered by a pro forma invoice or statement in the form of an invoice, and no forfeiture or disability of any kind incurred under the provisions of this section shall be remitted or mitigated by the Secretary of the Treasury. The duty shall not, however, be assessed in any case upon an amount less than the entered value, unless by direction of the Secretary of the Treasury in cases in which the importer certifies at the time of entry that the entered value is higher than the foreign market value and that the goods are so entered in order to meet advances by the appraiser in similar cases then pending on appeal for reappraisement, and the importer's contention shall subsequently be sustained by a final decision on reappraisement, and it shall appear that the action of the importer on entry was taken in good faith, after due diligence and inquiry on his part, and the Secretary of the Treasury shall accompany his directions with a statement of his conclusions and his reasons therefor.

Anti-dumping Paragraph Adopted by the House of Representatives in 1913.

The tariff bill of 1913 (H. R. 3321) as it passed the House of Representatives, contained in Section IV, paragraph R, this provision:

"That whenever articles are exported to the United States of a class or kind made or produced in the United States, if the export or actual selling price to an importer in the United States, or the price at which such goods are consigned is less than the fair market value of the same article when sold for home consumption in the usual and ordinary course in the country whence exported to the United States at the time of its exportation to the United States, there shall, in addition to the duties otherwise established, be levied, collected, and paid on such article on its importation into the United States a special duty (or dumping duty) equal to the difference between the said export or actual selling price of the article for export or the price at which such goods are consigned, and the said fair market value thereof for home consumption, provided that the said special duty shall not exceed 15 per centum ad valorem in any case and that goods whereon the duties otherwise established are equal to 50 per centum ad valorem shall be exempt from such special duty.

"'Export price' or 'selling price' or 'price at which such goods are consigned' in this section shall be held to mean and include the exporter's price for the goods, exclusive of all charges thereon after their shipment from the place whence exported directly to the United States.

"The Secretary of the Treasury shall make such rules and regulations as are necessary for the carrying out of the provisions of this section and for the enforcement thereof."

This book should be returned to the Library on or before the last date stamped below.

A fine of five cents a day is incurred by retaining it beyond the specified time.

Please return promptly.

CPSIA information can be obtained
at www.ICGtesting.com
Printed in the USA
LVHW082204151219
640618LV00009B/55/P